Extraordinary Praise for Celia Rivenbark and
We're Just Like You, Only Prettier

"Warm, witty, and wise, rather like reading dispatches from a friend who uses e-mail and still writes letters, in ink, on good paper."
—*St. Petersburg Times*

"What starts as a wry little snicker will grow into guffaws. . . . This book is not just for Southerners."—*The News of Orange County* (North Carolina)

"Will give you a case of the giggles."
—*New York Daily News*

"Indulge in a heaping helping of female fabulousness . . . a hilarious look at the world."
—*Complete Woman*

"An edgy Erma, an Erma dipped in corn bread batter, wrapped in collard greens, and drawling that she was speeding because 'My uterus told me to.'"
—*The Tennessean*

"A hoot and a holler."
—*Boston Herald*

"North Carolina doesn't have a post for a 'humorist laureate,' but it should invent one and install Celia Rivenbark. . . . But Rivenbark's interests go beyond the regional—and that's to her credit."
—*Greensboro News & Record*

"I loved Celia's book; it made me want to get myself a double-wide, head on down to Mama and them's, and start mowing my own lawn. I never knew that Southern folks had time aside from cooking the best food in the world to grow such marvelous senses of humor. For a Yankee like me, Southern life was always fascinating, but who knew it was so pants-wetting funny (except watching a hillbilly bang his head repeatedly on the door of the outhouse, because I've seen that, you know)? And there's also the mention of 'making doody,' which is always a shoo-in for me. Celia's book rocks; everyone is going to love it
    P.S.: How much prettier is she than me?"
—Laurie Notaro, author of *The Idiot Girls' Action Adventure Club*

"When the aliens come to study us, I hope they find Celia Rivenbark's work prominently displayed. She is one of our greatest domestic anthropologists, digging up and airing all those things we like to think others don't know. In other words, THE TRUTH. She knows the South and she knows women, but that's just the tip of it all. I think she might very well know EVERYTHING. I don't know when I have laughed so loud and so long. I am forever a devoted fan."
—Jill McCorkle, author of *Creatures of Habit*

ALSO BY CELIA RIVENBARK

Bless Your Heart, Tramp

WE'RE JUST LIKE YOU,

Only Prettier

CONFESSIONS OF A TARNISHED SOUTHERN BELLE

Celia Rivenbark

ST. MARTIN'S GRIFFIN ✤ NEW YORK

For Scott

www.stmartins.com

Library of Congress Cataloging-in-Publication Data

Rivenbark, Celia.
    We're just like you, only prettier : confessions of a tarnished southern belle / Celia Rivenbark. —1st ed.
        p.   cm.
    ISBN 0-312-31243-1 (hc)
    ISBN 0-312-31244-X (pbk)
    EAN 978-0312-31244-2
    1. Southern States—Social life and customs—Anecdotes.
2. Southern States—Social life and customs—Humor.
3. Rivenbark, Celia—Anecdotes.   4. Rivenbark, Celia—Humor.
5. Women—Southern States—Anecdotes.   6. Women—Southern
States—Humor.   7. American wit and humor.   I. Title.

F209.6.R58   2004
978—dc22

                                                2003058190

10 9 8 7 6 5 4 3

Contents

CONTENTS

Part 2: Kids
JUST BECAUSE THEY DON'T HAVE GILLS DOESN'T MEAN THEY'RE HUMAN

CONTENTS

Part 3: Couples Therapy, Southern Style
LORD, PLEASE DON'T LET ME KILL HIM TILL THE HOUSE IS PAID FOR

CONTENTS

Part 4: The Southern Woman
THE TRUTH? WE'RE JUST LIKE YOU, ONLY PRETTIER

CONTENTS

Part 5: The Gravy on the Grits
BOOBALICIOUS SPEAKS OUT!

CONTENTS

Introduction

I knew that native Southerners weren't like the rest of y'all, but after the publication of my first book, *Bless Your Heart, Tramp,* I became even more convinced that we're a great curiosity to others, a sort of collard-under-glass to be examined for our twisted roots, our ability to grow and flourish in uncertain soil, and, maybe more than anything, our amazing sweetness that only comes after experiencing drought or frost.

We are, like our beloved garden greens, sturdy, strong, and best when tested by the elements and fully seasoned. I never bought the notion of the "steel magnolia" because it's a short-lived, silly blossom that can't make it through a simple Women's Missionary Union meeting without shedding its powdery guts onto the mahogany sideboard.

No, we are collards. Green at times, tender at times, tough at times, and possessing great staying power.

At book signings and readings throughout the South, the Yankee transplants would raise their hands to ask for help in understanding the Southern lexicon. ("What is this 'we've howdied but not met'?" "What do you mean when you say 'this little junk o' mess'?" "Why do you say to 'sit down, the coffee's been saucered and blowed'?") They cornered me for heart-to-hearts about why we are so passionate about family silver, knowing whose people you "come from," why we are so much more fond of flowers from a friend's garden than those from the florist, and most particularly, the war we can't seem to move past. At one bookstore, a Yankee reader suggested that we simply "get over it." I summoned my smelling salts and launched into an attack of William Tecumseh Sherman (a horrible racist, don't forget) that made me sound a little like a crazy collard.

So, yes, I realized there was much more to be said about the South and the best way to say it, I figured, was to write a book that invites you to crawl inside our homes and families. There are all sorts of Southern characters in here, some real and some imagined, from the aged Auntie, who lives off Payday bars and pure misery at the rest home to the fresh-faced Amy, who makes the decidedly un-Southern mistake of wearing regular clothes all the way through her pregnancy. Bless her heart.

To be sure, some of the notions in this book are shared far beyond the South. I suspect, for instance, that the relationship between man and big screen knows no geographic boundary. And it's not just Southern sisters who are horrified when we must, through no fault of our own but only through the most dire and unforseeable awfulness, place the father in charge of dressing the children for the day. Verily, he will screw it up.

(On second thought, a Southern woman might care just a tad more about this botching of plaids and stripes, navy with "sort of" navy, because it's in our nature to agonize about such trivialities and no one does it better.)

A word of explanation: Many of these essays may not seem particularly Southern at all, but they are a Southern woman's take on those irksome little yuks in daily life, bringing our "half bubble off plumb" personalities to assorted horrors like kids' beauty pageants, birthing babies, and having to spend money on car maintenance instead of the root perm we so richly deserve.

This book is best enjoyed with the Allman Brothers *Eat a Peach* CD playing somewhere in the background and a plate of—what else?—collards and cornbread waiting for you at the supper table. The fatback is optional because, even here in the South, we've finally started obsessing over our cholesterol.

I cook my collards, these days, with low-sodium chicken broth and, oddly, this makes me feel more guilty than virtuous. Is this the beginning of the end? Am I going to become some sad lapsed belle who, in a struggle to blend in, forsakes all things intensely Southern, feeling odd embarrassment over treasured old rituals like taking the marshmallow-speckled lime gelatin mold to the grieving family? Will I stop shaving my underarms or padding my bra? Will I stop describing, as only a true Southerner can, a truly awful physical appearance as simply "most unfortunate" as in, "She has a most unfortunate nose"?

I pray not, because I don't want my daughter to grow up in a gray-sky South, a land of "you guys" replacing "y'all," a South as bland as a bowl of grits without the redeye gravy. No, no. That would lead to a most unfortunate life. I hope for the best of the South, all eccentricities reporting for duty, for my little collard sprout. And for yours, too, wherever they may grow.

Part 1:

THE SOUTHERN

Family

And No, We Don't Marry Our Cousins—
Unless, Of Course, They Got Cable

1

STOP WATCHING YOUR PLASMA TV
and Start Selling Your Plasma!

How to Become Honest-to-Jesus White Trash

I'm not sure when it happened but white trash is in. I just read it in a national magazine and all I could say was, "Well, shit fire and save the matches!"

You don't have to be Southern to be white trash, but it helps, mostly because Southerners know the beauty of a potted meat and mayonnaise sandwich better than most.

As a sort of on-the-bubble white trash girl myself (I've never, technically, had what car dealers describe as "bruised credit"), I'm feeling downright giddy.

Why is white trash chic now? Maybe it's just natural backlash to decades of greed and consumption. Whatever the reason, there's much to learn and I can coach even the snobbiest of y'all on how to be WT.

For starters, bad TV is a huge part of the WT lifestyle.

White trash women spend their last dime calling Miss Cleo at the Psychic Screw-You Network. It takes a WT brain to stare at the screen at the butt-crack o' dawn and say: "Hey, she's never met me and knows nothing about me but I bet this crazy island woman can tell me what my future will be."

Psychics are nothing new to country folk. When I was growing up, I can remember the weird Madame Isadora down the road who had a huge red palm billboard right in her front yard. Even as a tot I was skeptical of the abilities of a "psychic-heeler" (sic) who couldn't afford underpinning on her trailer.

Aside from psychic infomercials, WT never wants to miss those midnight monster-truck marathons. Hell, the young'uns can sleep through second period so just nail that satellite dish on the most prominent tree in your front yard. No trees? No problem. Just use your Confederate flagpole. Buy your descrambler from the mullet-headed guy who runs the cockfight behind the landfill.

Mullet-headed, you say?

The mullet is the WT man's hairstyle of choice. It's long in back, short on the sides, and kinda fluffy on top. Mullet men think this makes them look young, virile, and rather like an Alabama roadie instead of the double-wide salesmen they are in real life. Not that there's anything wrong with that.

Mullets, also known as the ape drape; the achy, breaky, big mistakey; and the Kentucky waterfall, are often favored by WT who are losing some hair on top. Curls flowing down their backs are not so much sissy as Samson.

Here's some other tips on being WT. Don't thank me now. Just give me one of the rottweiler pups when they're born and, yes, breeding 'em is too a real job.

Ladies, begin every sentence with "My baby's daddy." Even if you're married to him, it lends volumes of white trash cachet to a simple sentence. Yeah, it does.

Take to ending every declarative statement with "Yeah, it does." (Alternate acceptable WT: "I heard that.")

Take forty or fifty of your closest relatives to the emergency room with you every time one of you gets shot in the ass. This drives emergency personnel crazy but, hey! your tax dollars built this hospital. Well. They would have if you'd ever technically filed a tax return. Which of course white trash doesn't.

(Now on the matter of tax returns, if you do go high falutin' and file one, make sure you do *not* go to the classy accountant. You know the Edward Rothschild Ravensbottom firm with the picture of the old dude with the wooden dentures in the mahogany-paneled foy-yay. Choose instead the rather sad storefront Presto Fasto firm that shares office space with bad Chinese takeout and a "lingerie-modeling" agency.)

Dress your young'uns in little black NASCAR T-shirts but teach them to hate Jeff Gordon on account of he's just too damned pretty for his own good. Make sure you enter your girl young'uns in all the Wee Tiny Miss beauty pageants because it's the ultimate WT lifestyle to spend two weeks' salary on hair extensions and pancake makeup for your three-year-old just so she can win a five-dollar trophy and the adoration of, well, nobody much.

Take up smoking again and learn how to talk and smoke at the same time, preferably while saying hardcore white trash things like, "Ever since I got on the disability, I've had to do whatever I could to put food on the table. Your Honor."

Ladies, keep those bra straps hanging out on *both* sides, okay?

Drive the non-WTs crazy by going to the post office and buying *lots* of money orders. You don't need no stinkin' checking account. ("Let's see, here, I need one for fifty-eight dollars and twenty-one cents, one for sixty-two dollars and forty-four cents, that one goes to my choir-o-practor. . . .") Ask the postal clerk why they never have any stamps that say Hate. While you're there, ask the clerk the difference between certified and registered mail. Follow his painfully thorough three-minute response with the classic WT rebuttal: "Say who?"

If you're sincere about wanting to join America's trendiest new demographic, you gotta start buying lottery tickets, and lots of 'em. ("Keep scratching, Melva, the young'uns can eat mustard sandwiches another week or two.")

Of course, you don't have to be poor to be white trash. Not long ago, that point was proven by a couple of big-wig South Carolina politicians who argued the benefits of the lottery to a roomful of high school boys attending a leadership conference.

Democrat Dick Harpootlian told the boys that state lottery funds would provide up to $4,500 for college, and could "buy a lot of beer and girls," but he was countered by Republican Henry McMaster who pointed out that while Democrats are for beer and girls, "Republicans are for cold beer and hot girls."

And all this time, I just thought they were for a bunch of boring stuff like wilderness drilling, silly missile shields that don't work, and protecting tax breaks for the stupefyingly rich.

Just so the whole thing wouldn't get too partisan, Mr. Harpootlian summed things up by saying that while the parties disagree in principles, they certainly "agree on beer and girls."

Mr. McMaster said he was just using humor to grab the teens' attention before discussing issues like gun control and education.

I don't see this as a natural segue, myself. ("After a

tough night of paying for sex and getting knee-walking drunk, I like to contemplate the legal and ethical arguments behind our right to bear arms and, if'n I'm especially wall-eyed, I like to ponder the philosophical and moral arguments of the school voucher system or increased charter-school funding versus the moral obligation not to abandon our failing inner-city schools.")

Say who?

Maybe Harpootlian and McMaster can speak to Girls State and say something equally insightful about cold beer and hot guys. I'll bet those Bush twins, Fluffy and Muffy, who have a notoriously hard time just saying no to a margarita or three would appreciate that. Yeah, they would.

Politicians of all races have a lot of white trash in them. They have to rein themselves in, is all.

Not too long ago in my state, Elizabeth Dole (separated at birth from the Joker from *Batman* although I don't have actual proof) was running for the United States Senate against a fellow named—and I am not making this up—Erskine Bowles.

They both started out their campaigns by saying they wouldn't buy "attack ads." But that was then, and this is two weeks before the election.

Not long before Dole won, I turned on the TV in time to hear her say, "Oh, yeah? Well, *your mama!*" to

Bowles, who replied with, *"Your greasy grandma!"*

Or words to that effect.

It's fun to see how money and influence can make things seem more polished but, deep down, once white trash, always white trash.

In high school, if you didn't like the candidate for student council president, you could just trip him when he walked by.

In the big leagues, tripping is frowned on so there is a "war chest" of campaign money that is raised and spent. This money represents small contributions from concerned individuals from across this great land. Oh, I crack myself up. This money comes from corporate fat cats who want their candidate to vote in ways that will benefit the fat cats. This is known as busting one's erskines.

The interesting thing about political campaign ads down South is that, because we are considered by the fat cats from other parts of the country to be, well, stupid, they will hire a very non-white-trash-sounding spokesman for the commercials.

His buttery voice will ooze behind a backdrop of imported bumpkins who look just like real people, only slightly hickier.

See, the irony is the candidate wants the white trash vote but doesn't want to seem white trash himself or herself.

The real fun begins with the "counterattack ads," which are designed to confuse the voters even more.

Voice of solemn announcer: "Liddy Dole plans to take all of your hard-earned social security money to Atlantic City and gamble it all on the Big Wheel, nickel slots, and Penn and Teller tickets."

Voice of counterattack ad announcer: "Erskine Bowles was Bill Clinton's Chief of Staff."

Voice of solemn announcer: "Liddy Dole led the fight against raising minimum wage, thus ensuring that you would never be able to afford a better life for yourself or your children."

Voice of counterattack announcer: "Erskine Bowles is ugly and his mama dresses him funny. Oh, and he worked for Bill Clinton."

Solemn announcer again: "Liddy Dole hates being called Liddy and that's why we keep doing it in these ads."

Voice of counterattack announcer: "Erskine is a dumb name. The kind of name a man who cheated on his wife while president might like."

It would be wrong to imply that white trash politicians are limited to the South. Minnesota governor Jesse Ventura embodied many of the fine white trash traditions of all of us who have lived, at one time or another, on a chassis.

Yeah, he did.

2

BABY BORN
Won't Poop

How a Constipated Doll Baby Sabotaged the Hap-Hap-Happiest Time of the Year

The scene on Christmas Day afternoon was straight out of a Norman Bates, er, Rockwell, portrait. There we all were: me, my husband, and our three-year-old, lovingly surrounded by assorted grandmothers, uncles, aunts, and cousins all staring, rapt, at the festively decorated dining table.

And there, in the center of the table, was no pineapple beringed ham or golden turkey but rather a foot-tall baby doll balanced, but barely, on a too-small pink plastic potty.

"Why won't she go?" my brother-in-law moaned. He stepped forward and began to squeeze, pinch, and then pound Baby Born on her pink potty.

Aunts who had helped feed the doll, my daughter's only Santa request "because she performs seven boddiddy fun-shuns," stood back and clucked their tongues.

"Maybe she needs some prunes," one finally said, apparently serious.

The brother-in-law continued to pound Baby Born up and down on her potty. Saliva was now dripping from both corners of his mouth and his eyes gleamed like Jack Nicholson's in *The Shining.*

Baby Born had taken over our holiday and made us all a little crazy. She is made of hard plastic, has slightly maniacal blue eyes, and isn't even fun to hold. She was one of the most in-demand toys that Christmas, leading me to realize that our wacky dining table scene was probably being repeated in hundreds of thousands of American households.

Baby Born came with instructions that you should only feed her the specially formulated cereal (sample packets included) before sitting her on her magic pink potty and waiting for nature, or something like it, to take its course.

There was a warning: "If Baby Born does not go on her potty, push her down and hold her in position until she is finished. *Do not let go!"*

I could only imagine what horror would ensue if we let go, so, like paramedics doing CPR, one member of the family would hold on to Baby Born until they got tired and another would take over immediately.

As my brother-in-law continued to pound away, my daughter began to cry.

"You're *hurting* her," she wailed.

"Don't—be—ridiculous," he panted through clenched teeth. His voice got all high and squeaky then. "Baby Born likes the trampoline jump, don't you, Baby Born, don't you? Oh, yes um do."

Okay, so he'd lost his mind.

With several aunts taking turns, we decided to try to get Baby Born to at least cry real tears As Seen on TV.

When she couldn't even do that, I felt like crying a few of my own. For damned near fifty bucks, Baby Born should perform at least two of the seven fun-shuns.

"Seven?" my husband mused. "That's more than I got, I'm pretty sure." The aunts laughed at this so he said it a few more times.

The instructions advised that Baby Born would need to be rinsed frequently so she "would not be allowed to grow moldy inside."

Oh, great. Instead of a precious doll for my daughter to cuddle with at night, I was going to wrap her arms around a fungal, constipated, and vastly overpriced piece of plastic.

The instructions further advised that, in the event of a blockage, you should "shake her vigorously in all directions, set her on the special potty, and repeat the entire procedure several times." Note to self: Postpone life.

We worked on this until late into the evening. Finally, six hours behind schedule, we sat down to a proper Christmas dinner. At my daughter's tearstained request, Baby Born sat in her own chair, smirking I thought, as her place at the table meant the brother-in-law had to balance his plate on a tiny Hollie Hobbie TV tray that one of the aunts found rusting behind the dryer.

I believe that if he could have, he would've taken Baby Born for a long ride into the country that cold December night.

Over the next few months, we tried, in vain, to get Baby Bitch, as I took to calling her, to do anything at all except sit there and look snotty.

She didn't pee or poop, she didn't cry "real tears," she didn't squeal "Bah!" when you lifted her arm (pumping vigorously according to the directions). She didn't do shit.

The directions were very specific about never giving Baby Born anything but water in her useless specially designed bottle. Lemonade, tea, or "even milk" would damage the "intricate interior workings" of the doll.

One day my daughter and her little friend were giving Baby Born some orange juice, although I'd told them she could only have water. She had so much damned water sloshing in her now that she sounded like a coconut when you shook her. Which I had taken to doing a lot lately.

"What are you doing!" I shrieked. "You know she's not supposed to have juice. It will make her sticky inside!"

"So what?" my daughter asked.

"Good point. Carry on."

I have no idea where Baby Born is at this moment. Presumably she's sitting around in her permanent squat position, full of mushy cereal, OJ, and water. Which, now that I think about it, sounds just like my aunt Sudavee before she went to the home.

This Christmas, my daughter is angling for something called the "Make Me Pretty Talking Styling Head." You tote it around by the hair and adorn its pretty face with makeup and curl its pretty hair, but, at the end of the day, it still looks like what it is, a severed head.

She's also asked for something called the Fisher-Price Loving Family Home & Stable. I don't really get the stable connection unless you're supposed to pretend that if daddy comes home feeling less than loving, the little plastic family can retreat to the stable.

My daughter's wish list is very long this year, perhaps because she has learned that one lousy toy can wreck your whole holiday. So, as insurance, she's asked for two popular dolls: Bratz and Divas, which really gives me new hope for her generation. ("What do you want to be when you grow up? A brat or a diva?" Of course, the inevitable answer is the same: "Britney.")

She's also asked for a "kiddy recliner." They're hot this

year, but I don't get it. Isn't there some dues-paying that has to be done here? You can't just turn four and get a recliner to relax in after a tough day of finger painting and playing army.

Nope, you have to earn a recliner, preferably after working many thankless years for an abusive boss who is as innovative as drain hair.

Christmas can be excessive at our house, but I'm still not ready to follow the advice of those killjoys at *Money* magazine who advise us to "shop sensibly" and "avoid debt." Why don't they just "bite me"?

Obviously these folks have never put off their kids' immunizations so they could use the money to buy more icicle lights at Wal-Mart.

Oh, calm down. When's the last time you actually *knew* someone with typhus? I thought so.

I suspect these fancy-ass writers for *Money* are the kind of people who put portabello mushrooms in their stuffing instead of giblets or, worse, drink likker to celebrate our Lord's birth.

They probably all live in fabulous clapboard houses in Connecticut, wear sweaters from Barney's that they paid too much for, and love to tell funny little inside jokes about pork-belly futures.

What makes them the experts? A few diplomas from some so-called Ivy League school, a high six-figure salary, and a bony ol' trophy wife?

Gosh, I hope that doesn't sound bitter.

It's just that when it comes to Christmas, you're not supposed to be safe and sensible. If God had wanted us to be sensible, he wouldn't have invented a food dehydrator that can make one hundred pounds of beef jerky in minutes, the singing bird clock ("Honey! We're gonna be late; it's already half past the sparrow's ass!"), or Bigmouth Billy Bass, the Singing Rubber Fish.

You can follow the magazine's holiday "tips" or use my real-world suggestions in parentheses. Don't thank me now. Thank me on December 25, preferably with a gaily wrapped gift that cost way more than it should and sent you spiraling into good old-fashioned proud-to-be-an-American 18.5 percent APR debt.

1. Make a list. Ask yourself if everyone truly belongs on the list. (Sure, I could cut out my high school friend that I haven't seen in two decades, but she's sweet as a Harry & David tangelo and she's the only person in North America who still thinks I weigh one hundred and ten pounds.)
2. Set limits. As you're making your list, write down a maximum dollar limit and stick to it. (Okay, I'm renewing my subscription to *Money* but I'm only paying you three bucks. How do *you* like it?)

3. Be realistic. Buy only gifts that you can afford
   to buy with cash. (Fine by me. What will it
   be for you, Big Red or Juicy Fruit?)
4. Trim expenses by making some presents
   yourself. (That's fine for those of you who
   have never had to tell a paramedic, "See, I
   borrowed my neighbor's glue gun. . . .")
5. Buy in bulk: A case of wine, elegant candles,
   or tins of homemade cookies also make great
   hostess gifts. (You call this sensible? How
   about a twelve-pack, some Bic lighters, and
   some delicious homemade beef jerky? I've got
   plenty, you know.)

3

THERE'S A HAIR
in My Bacon Grease

**Why the Greatest Generation Is Rinsing Out Ziploc
Bags and Eating Ptomaine Turkey**

I think Tom Brokaw said it best when describing the "Greatest Generation": Why can't any of y'all throw out leftovers?

Okay, maybe it was me, not Tom, who said that, but it's a question that comes to mind often, especially around the holidays when my seventy- and eighty-something friends lovingly scrape a single tablespoon of pearl onion casserole into a Tupperware container "for later."

Waste not, want, oh, I forget how it goes.

Don't get me wrong. I adore my older friends. As I write this, my eighty-one-year-old neighbor is on his roof cleaning out the gutters. I'm just praying that when he finishes, he'll offer to do mine. It's chilly out, you know.

So, yes, I get the whole war-surviving, Depression-dealing-with business, but what I don't get is why somebody who had a $35 monthly house payment and bought Circuit City stock for a quarter a share is still cleaning and refolding used tin foil and washing out the Ziploc bags.

My husband's aunt once salvaged a piece of mayonnaise-speckled Saran Wrap I had tossed into the trash. She spent a good five minutes sponging it clean again and gave me a look that said I knew nothing of ten-mile walks to school, uphill, both ways, with rickets.

The Greatest Generation refuses to throw away disposable cups. Just watch them. Oh, I know. We "young folks" are squandering our natural resources. Truly, great majestic forests of Solo-party-cup–producing red, yellow, and blue plastic are disappearing faster than pierceable body parts on a Gen X-er.

For some time now, I've realized that the Greatest Generation has the Greatest Gastrointestinal Tract.

How else do you explain how a very senior citizen can eat and enjoy a three-week-old piece of pork roast with no ill effects while it would send a younger person straight to the emergency room and a close call with the white light?

My friend knows better than to eat her grandmother's food. The woman has been known to thaw, cook, and refreeze a turkey until the poor bird finally just sits up on what's left of its freezer-burned haunches and screams to be put out of its misery.

My friend Merleen's mama-in-law, like every Southern woman of a certain age, even saves her bacon grease in a fancy little jar she made in ceramics that says Drippings and has hand-painted trolls dancing around under a mushroom tree.

As a newlywed, Merleen visited her mother-in-law and, being painfully eager to make a good impression, offered to clean up the kitchen. That's when her mother-in-law caught her pouring the bacon grease into an old mayonnaise jar and tossing it into the trash.

What happened next was a blur but Merleen said her mama-in-law's reaction was swift.

From the sound of it, she couldn't have been more shocked or hurt if she'd personally witnessed Merleen doing the devil's aerobics with the minister of music right there on her new Congoleum.

She sprang like a cheetah across the kitchen, rescued the bacon grease, and, holding it tenderly as a newborn, slowly poured the still-warm contents back into the Drippings jar.

The Greatest Generation often sniffs conspiracy where there is none.

At the KFC, my elderly friend narrowed her eyes when told there was "no dark meat available at the moment."

"You don't have *any* dark meat?" she asked, eyes narrowed and sizing up the Gen Y-er in front of her.

Her tone implied that there had been some sort of dark-meat conspiracy and the employees were in the back juggling thighs and drumsticks and joyfully spitting in the coleslaw.

We left and moved on to McDonald's where I was berated for forgetting to order the "Senior Coke."

"I don't know why you don't just slow down and throw that twenty cents out onto the highway," she huffed. "And where's my Senior Fish Sandwich?"

"It's chicken," I said wearily. "They were all out of fish."

"I'll just *bet* they were."

Sometimes I am aware that I'm turning into my grandmother. I'm becoming one of "them."

Yesterday, I screeched to my ten-year-old friend who had joined us for lunch that I'd give him a quarter if he'd take my kid to the gumball machine so I could complete the head-imploding task of calculating the tip.

The boy looked distressed while I, once again, screamed "Where's my purse?!" (and, yes, it was in my lap) and then he quietly informed me that I'd given him a nickel. Oh, well. It's so dad-gum dark in restaurants these days.

I've also discovered as I age, less than gracefully, that I have no patience.

The other day, as I stood in the "twenty items and under" checkout at the new Slap-Yo-Mama-Fine Super Wal-Mart, I grew increasingly irritated. It's supposed to be faster but it isn't because it allows all kinds of credit and debit swiping and swooshing and Español and whatnot. No one actually pays with cash money anymore, like when I was a girl. I know this because I gave the cashier a twenty-dollar bill and she looked at it, puzzled, like it was badly aged lettuce.

Before that, I'd tried three lines that turned out to be not moving at all. They were, apparently, faux checkouts. Wal-Mart seems to have more of these than anybody else. People who look like real customers stand for hours at a time talking with people who look like real cashiers but no one actually moves.

Sometimes, you'll stand in line forever and this one goober will come to the end of a long line, then jump in front when a new register is opened.

I had a fight with a line-jumper last week, having invested fifteen minutes in a nonmoving line. A new register opened and he walked right up. I ran over, dropped to all fours, and started gnawing on his pants leg, pulling him slowly away from the register.

"You're a nut," he said, backing away.

"Fair's fair," I mumbled through his pants leg.

Recently, I had the misfortune to get behind a giggly, cute young couple who, oopsie, had selected the only frozen turkey in Wal-Mart that had neither weight nor price on it. I waited and watched my nails grow until the perky girlfriend arrived, triumphant, with the newly weighed turkey. I scowled and considered wearing my bedroom shoes to the store next time because they're so much more comfortable.

Later on, Cute Couple blocked my car with their cart while they took turns hopping on the back of it and pretending to steer one another on a sled. It was so cute, so joyous, so young-and-in-love. It really pissed me off.

"Hey, Mork and Mindy," I sniped, "get a room!"

I've become the Hallmark crone. And I *like* it. Can washing the Chinet really be far behind?

4

MAMA AND THEM,
Precious and Dahlin'

Why The Sopranos *Could Never Survive Down South*

*T*o *someone* from up North, the expression "Mama and them" is an oddity, guaranteed to earn the exact same look I got after asking the nice man at Bergdorf's to "mash nine" when I was on vacation in New York.

Who is "them," the Yankee wonders whilst fingering his gold chains or meditatively spinning his pinkie diamond.

In the South, "them" is Daddy, usually, but it can also encompass every bony-ribbed yard cat that might be hanging around at the time or whatever siblings and assorted Aunt Ola Mays or Pee Paws or Mee Maws might be found rocking on the porch now and again.

To the newcomer to the South, hearing that a co-worker plans a weekend visit to "Mama and them's" (the correct plural possessive, don'tchaknow), might make him think that Mama has been left alone either through an act of scoundreldom involving the town's resident hoochie-mama (an altogether different kind of mama) or Daddy's untimely demise.

Not so. That's "and them's" truck out front and "and them" is busily working in the cucumber patch or repairing a dresser drawer when you arrive for a visit, just like he always is.

"And them's" very first words to you are always the same: "Your mama's in the house." It is said with love, of course. If there were any other response, your visit to the Southern homeplace would be completely cattywumpus, as crazy as if you'd come in to find the whole family, including Uncle Snookie, sitting at the kitchen table sprinkling sugar on their grits.

I adore "Mama and them." The day it disappears from the Southern lexicon is the day we will find ourselves giving cash money for wedding presents instead of going to the Belk bridal registry like God intended and trying to explain—again—that "all you gotta do, Gee-mama, is just touch the screen!"

To assume that "Mama and them" is a dissing of Daddy would be as wrongheaded as watching *Wheel of Fortune* when you know the Billy Graham crusade is on another channel at the very same time.

It's intensely Southern to feel guilty when Billy's on

and you're not watching. And now we gotta worry about Franklin, too, with his good-looking self.

But you know what Franklin Graham says when he's planning to visit his famous folks for the weekend? "Let's go to Mama and them's."

I guarantee it, hons.

In general, Yankees are perpetually amused and confused by Southernspeak and Southern ways.

The other night, while watching *The Sopranos*, it hit me like a truck of stolen Sonys: TV's favorite mobster family would wither on the vine like an overripe muskmelon if they lived down South.

For starters, there's no way they'd be allowed to talk "ugly," as my great-aunt Raylene would say. Plus, there's no way they'd fit in around here wearing those silk shirts and shiny pompadours.

Weekly "waste-management" staff meetings at The Cracker Barrel instead of beloved turnpike strip joint Bada Bing? I don't think so, paisan.

Oh, and the Sopranos would hate the food down here.

They're always gushing about traditional Italian fare, stuff like "ree-coat" pie and "can-*oh*-lees." They always tank up on enormous messy meals like mussels marinara right before a hit. Chicken and pastry, Southern-style, just wouldn't cut it. You can't shoot a guy full of holes on okra and tomatoes and spoon bread. No, you eat Southern food and you just want to hug your mama and take a nap on the divan, a baseball game turned down low in the background.

On *The Sopranos*, the Yankee men kiss each other's cheeks all the time. They arrive to play golf together, they kiss; they go for a stroll on the boardwalk and an egg cream (?), they kiss. I get that it's because they're "family," less Waltons than Manson to be sure, but it still looks "quair" as they say in the South, and would earn some unpleasant stares at Bubba's Brew 'n' Cue.

Carmela Soprano would never fit in at the monthly DAR meetings, what with her fell-off-the-back-of-a-truck diamond, department store sterling, painted-on capris, and tacky-ass teased upsweep.

Their names aren't Southern, either. Bonpensiero, Altieri, Aprile, Dante, Cifaretto, Moltisanti . . . not a single Ravenel or Pinckney or Blanchard among 'em.

No, the Sopranos wouldn't last long down here, offering "thirty large" for a stolen Lexus and swilling Chianti on the corner with the other "made" guys. Around here, we buy American and we drink Cheerwine with our checkers.

The accents would pose a problem, too, for Sopranos down South.

In the South, you see, everything is "just precious and dahlin'." The designation of "just the most precious thing" is frequently used to describe everything from an attentive and dutiful daughter-in-law to a particularly memorable roasted chicken purchased at the Piggly Wiggly deli.

Certainly, we could offer remedial courses for the many transplants we have welcomed from Sopranoland.

In fact, according a recent survey, a Southern accent is actually better than a New Jersey one if you're applying for a job. While the study found that Southerners were passed over for top-level jobs, they did get hired for midlevel jobs, while Jerseyites were most likely to find only low-level employment.

At long last, we have common ground. I would have bet the 'baccy farm that Southerners would finish dead last in a survey like that. For years we have been portrayed in the media as several pickles shy of a quart, all because of our slow, melodious drawl. But now, we discover that Gomer and Goober would get the job quicker than Tony and Paulie Walnuts. Oy!

Not to worry. New Jersey folk can improve their chances of getting a better-paying job by pretending to be Southern. May I suggest Southern speech classes filled with Yankees dutifully chanting phrases such as "It's so dry, the trees are a-bribin' the dawgs!"

(Pop quiz question: "What phrase is almost always the last thing a redneck good ol' boy says before he dies?" Answer: "Hey, y'all! Watch this!")

For extra credit, you could go outside and either fry a turkey or fire off a tater gun with a can of Aqua Net.

Despite classes, though, Tony Soprano and Co. would never understand the mind and soul of the good ol' boy. Just recently, I read the sad-but-true story of a GOB who choked to death on a live perch after grabbing it from the water and dropping it headfirst into his mouth.

While I have the utmost respect for a man who can catch fish with his bare hands, I wish he'd just dredged it in cornmeal and fried it like he was supposed to. Authorities concluded that the man had been drinking all afternoon and alcohol may have played a role in the fishy fatality.

Everybody say duh-huh.

The mob wives wouldn't fit in any better than their murdering husbands. While Carmela Soprano and her tacky gal-pals tend to go to spinning class and get seaweed wraps between baking "mani-*cote*" and such, Southern women are, frankly, harder working. We are obsessively devoted to horticulture and far more aware of natural beauty. We aren't ashamed to have dirt from the garden embedded in the prongs of our 3-carat diamond engagement rings.

The profoundly Southern woman will slam on the brakes of her Grand Cherokee to point out a particularly magnificent pink dogwood or mourn evidence of blight.

A Yankee friend of mine once remarked that the one

thing she couldn't understand was why so many South-ern women mow their own grass.

Well, of course we do. We are precious and dahlin' in our straw mowing hats. And don't you forget it, sugah.

5

HERE COMES *the Bride*

***Let's Just Get 'Em Hitched Sometime
Before We See the Head***

Is it small wonder that hurricane season and wedding season are one and the same? As a former bridal-page editor, I can honestly say that I've seen some category 5 wedding disasters.

Take the bride whose write-up included the delectable morsel that "She entered the church on the arm of her father while singing an a cappella rendition of 'All of Me' dedicated to her groom."

And then there was the infamous friend of a friend of mine who hired some silky singers to croon "Once, Twice, Three Times a Lady" as the processional for her third wedding.

I adore weddings. The families, the emotion, the beautiful gowns, the sacredness, the little honey-sesame chicken wings . . .

I fulfilled a lifelong dream a while back—directing a wedding—when a friend looked desperately into my eyes, and said, "I don't have a lot of money to waste on this so will you do it for free?" I was touched.

Because weddings make me bawl (in one friend's video, the only sounds you can hear are my wailing and the sound of the groom's ninety-year-old mom's oxygen tank clicking away), I was a little hesitant. Only one thing would cure my jitters: power "har."

On the morning of the wedding, I had my har teased so high in front I looked like Jimmy Swaggert in a blue crepe sheath (which I suspect he owns and trots out just for "special friends").

With big har, you don't snivel and bawl, you say things one time and everyone scurries to do your bidding. It's fabulously empowering. ("Hey! Move that candelabrum two inches to the left. No? *Do you see my hair?* That's better, asshole.")

When the groom's mother, a ferocious-looking woman with big har of her own, arrived a full forty-five minutes late (and wearing one of those god-awful glassy-eyed mink stoles where the little minks are chasing themselves around your throat), I was calm but firm.

"Hon," I said sweetly, "since we've already heard every song your thirteen-year-old nephew knows on the piano, including 'The Ballad of the Green Beret' and 'Drop Kick Me, Jesus (Through the Goalposts of Life),' what say you move your minks right on down the aisle and we'll get these two hitched sometime before we see the head."

Well, I didn't say she was a classy friend, now, did I?

No one has asked me to direct a wedding since and I place the blame squarely on the taxidermied shoulders of the mother of the groom.

Or perhaps it's because couples aren't taking marriage as seriously as they used to.

Just the other day, I read about the trend of the "starter marriage." That's the catchy label for marriages that last less than five years, take place in your twenties or early thirties, and end with no kids and little regret.

Starter marriages are all the rage these days, partly because you don't have to give back any of the wedding gifts. You stuck out holy matrimony for sixty months, for heaven's sake. Think of it as a typical car-payment coupon book and now you can, ahem, trade up.

Sure, you may have married a metaphorical drunk bike the first time, but a Lexus could be just around the corner, complete with global positioning system technology. Oh, I'm getting misty here!

According to the experts, the breakup of the typical starter marriage should be amicable. Aside from some predictable squabbling about who's going to get the Krups retro toaster, everybody usually stays friends.

And that, hons, is where it gets weird, if you ask me.

The amicable divorce is an urban legend. You believe there's such a thing? Then you also believe that some loser really did find an entire fried chicken head in his KFC snack pak.

Simply stated: Thou shalt not be friends with thy ex. It's, well, icky.

I know people who claim to be friends with their ex-spouses and I always tell 'em that I'd rather eat my own eyeballs than be friends with my ex. It's nothing personal, it's just that you can't buddy up with somebody who has seen you slough the dead skin off your heels. In bed.

While there's certainly no need to be mean to an ex-spouse, there's also no need to invite them to your parties in some misguided attempt to show everybody how danged civilized you are.

Freak: "Oh, look, there's Joel! Yoo-hoo! Jo-*el*! I'm so glad you could make it tonight! And who's your friend? She's absolutely stunning!"

Normal Person: "Oh, look, there's Joel. That lying sack of shit. Who's the cheap Christmas trash hanging all over him? Wait a minute. I'll just go say hello. Hi, Joel. Have you told Lil' Kim here that you still wet the bed?"

Allow me to remind you that we're not talking about people with children here. If you've made babies with somebody, you have to at least be civil during those

McDonald's drop-offs for the sake of the lil puddins who didn't ask to be brought into any of your midlife angst crap.

But if you're both free and clear, I say move on and don't look back.

On a gut level, the whole starter marriage concept is a bit offensive, particularly to an aspiring professional wedding directress like me.

After all, you're supposed to be entering a sacred union with your partner for life. Getting married shouldn't be like checking another item off your postcollege to-do list like taking up yoga or switching to decaf.

Marriage has been on my mind a lot lately because Paul McCartney just got remarried to a small child.

Okay, not really; she's thirty-four and he's sixty, but I'm still somewhat over it.

Paul's kids, who are roughly the same age as his new bride, dutifully attended the wedding but they looked like they'd been sucking on lemons, perhaps pondering the wisdom of dad marrying a woman who posed nude for a fund-raising calendar. Strangely, the bride's family looked joyous.

Of course, there's nothing wrong with marrying your soul mate number two, and if she happens to be young and gorgeous, so much the better! Statistically speaking, it's almost impossible for billionaires to discover that their soulmates are fifty-five and restocking the shampoo end caps at Kmart.

Besides, there are countless examples of these May-December romances working out. Anna Nicole Smith, who married a very wealthy fossil, won the right to keep some of her (very) hard-earned millions despite protests from the fossil's seventy-something tot who claimed she only married dad for the money. The cad!

I don't have anything against Paul's new bride. After all, she's going to have to live with a man who, while unspeakably rich and still cute, actually fires employees if he finds out they're meat eaters.

I always thought it was Linda, bless her heart, who had the whole family living off nuts and berries like a bunch of sunken-cheeked Unabombers. To tell you the truth, when Linda died, I figured Paul would return to his senses and go straight from the funeral home to the Wendy's drive-thru, where he'd order a triple with cheese, licking his fingers and dancing about like a mad-man. My bad. As it turns out, the worker bees who had to erect the tents and so forth for Paul's $3.2 million wedding to Heather Mills were fired if they so much as smuggled in a ham sandwich in their lunch pails.

Paul is so antimeat that only a vegetarian reception was allowed. Fortunately, he did this at a remote Irish castle instead of here in the South. Just try having a wedding reception around here without a sausage ball or those little cocktail weenies in chili sauce and grape jelly and see how quickly you get bad-mouthed.

Sure, she's young, smart, and beautiful, and has married one of the richest men in the world but when Heather gets a hankerin' for pot roast and gravy, she's going to have to hide out in the loo. Plus, Paul *is* responsible for that horrible "We're So Sorry, Uncle Albert" song ("little, little gypsy girdle, get around!"). Nope, life isn't going to be a bed of McCartney roses for Miss Heather, so let's wish 'em luck, mates.

Celebrities have a hard time making marriage work. Remember how everybody wondered if Bill and Hillary would get a divorce?

While everybody else thought their problems were rooted in Bill's penchant for "trashy" women who wore too much makeup and could shoot pool with their toes, I knew there was something else wrong: too many houseguests.

In fourteen months, the Clintons had 404 overnight guests. Now, as someone who believes in the adage that fish and houseguests should be tossed out after three days, I can see that this could ruin any marriage.

The good news was that the guests donated some $625,000 to Hillary's Senate campaign. Hey, I consider myself lucky if any of my deadbeat overnight guests show up with a box of Krispy Kremes for breakfast.

It's easy to see how having 404 overnight guests could strain a marriage. When my husband's middle-aged, unmarried cousin (think Randy Quaid's character in *National Lampoon's Vacation*) showed up to stay with us recently, it was the longest fourteen hours of my life. ("I've got just a little laundry here. No rush, just when you've got the time.")

Sure, the Clintons lived in a big house but you're never quite yourself when there's a strange person flushing and unwrapping those little presidential-seal toothbrushes down the hall. It's unlikely that Bill and Hillary could have any time for amorous pursuits knowing that Steven Spielberg and the missus were in the next room probably making their bazillioneth kid together.

Money, along with overnight guests, is what trips up most marriages. The trouble can start as early as when the blissed-out couple goes to pick out the engagement ring.

Remember, gentlemen? After a nice spiel from the salesman about the four C's of diamond buying, she went straight for the much pricier emerald cuts where you realized you were about to get acquainted with the one B of diamond buying: bankruptcy.

So keeping in mind that, to a diamond salesman, the only real C that's important is "commission," you discreetly managed to inform him that you rent your furniture.

Crisis averted; return to the seven-chip clusters, which are "making a comeback!"

Later on, gents, the women will begin to whine for an "eternity band," which is the ring in the commercial that shows the husband renting a whole movie theater to show home movies to his wife chronicling their fabulous life together. He is hated by normal husbands everywhere.

If you do give an eternity band, for heaven's sake, get the one with the diamonds all the way around, not just on top. What does that mean? "I'll be with you for, well, half an eternity, sugar booger"?

Honesty, along with that diamond upgrade, will keep a marriage together.

A recent poll found that 40 percent of Americans keep secrets from their spouses and, most of the time, it's about how much money they spend.

What is wrong with you people? Don't you realize that the foundation of a successful, vibrant marriage is complete honesty? That anything less is demeaning and destructive to your relationship? I know, I know. Sometimes I crack myself up.

Here's some advice. (Heather, put down that kielbasa and listen up!) I haven't told my husband a truthful price on any personal or household item in more than a decade. Don't get me wrong. He's not the kind to carp about money, it's just that it's no fun to say, "Look at my new coat, love dump. I paid full price for it and it wasn't really worth it and I'm not even sure I like it all that much."

My standard answer to the straightforward "man" question of "How much did it cost?" is always the same: a quickly-muttered-while-leaving-the-room "Oh, not that much." To prevent a follow-up question—the dreaded "How much is 'not that much'?"—it's a good idea to say something to immediately change the subject such as, "Lord! Is that beetle larvae in your ear?" Works every time.

According to the survey, men and women lie to each other in equal numbers about spending habits. Your coat is his fish finder. Women also tend to hide purchases, usually clothing, then bring it out weeks later, and say, "This? I've had this old thing for ages, you big silly! Now are you going to get that larvae checked out or not?"

A friend recently confided that her husband lied to her about the price of a T-shirt he bought at a rock concert because he was afraid that she would be mad at him. He said the band had tossed the shirts to the audience during the encore but she found a credit-card receipt for the shirt in his jeans pocket the next day.

"Can you believe he'd do that?" she huffed. "I mean, if he wants to spend twenty bucks on a Pantera T-shirt while I'm over here clipping coupons for thirty-five cents off Prego, what business is that of mine? I'm just the wife, after all."

Okay, so she's pretty scary.

More interesting findings of this survey of one thousand men and women: Only 2 percent of them said they lied to a spouse about having an affair and 16 percent admitted they wished they could wake up and not be married anymore.

Not me. But occasionally I do wish I could wake up and not be lactose intolerant anymore. Hey, you have your dreams, I'll have mine.

6

WHERE WERE *YOU* When Stringbean Passed?

A Real Southerner Would Know the Answer to That Question

Southerners are preoccupied with death. As far back as I can remember, news of the recently dead was the number-one topic at any get-together. I have friends who can spend a solid forty-five minutes eulogizing a fifth cousin twice removed (don't ask me removed from what) without coming up for air.

When I go back home and bump into old friends and family, the conversation almost always starts with a recitation of the near or recently dead and disintegrates into sputtering frustration when it's obvious I have no idea who they're talking about.

"Of course you remember Boddie Sue. She was the one who wrote a fan letter to Stringbean and he wrote back that one time but then he got shot in the chest and died when those robbers broke into his house."

"What?"

"Oh, for heaven's sake, don't you remember String-bean on *Hee Haw*? Lord, missy, where did you spend the seventies anyway?"

"I don't know. Seventh grade?"

Maybe because we're all adults now, we're expected to know all the players.

"You *know* Pearlie and don't say you don't! Remember how he used to live down from Cousin Maynard's house and everybody always said he wouldn't amount to much because he had a crazy eye?"

I don't even remember Cousin Maynard, let alone the pitiful soul with the wandering eye that apparently could keep an eye on the front door while the other eye amused itself with the *TV Guide* crossword puzzle.

It's a small-town thing, perhaps, but when you reach your forties, you no longer greet one another at the Wal-Mart with "How are you?" Nope. You always start with a hushed and ominous, "Well, I guess you heard about Maudie. . . ."

The news that follows generally falls into two categories. Either Maudie has abandoned her husband and children and run off with the repo man at the Rent-a-Center or she's gone to that great double-wide in the sky, where the streets are paved with asphalt and all the men pay their child support on time and you don't even have to "garish" their wages, as my friend Petey-Lou calls it.

Petey-Lou swears she let the good one get away.

"Sure, all he done all day was smoke pot and watch *Gunsmoke*," she said wistfully, "but I think it's just 'cause he just loved Festus."

Sometimes, the trip back home is to "funeralize," something Southerners love to do because funeral food is so good. I've always thought that people who died in July are the most thoughtful because you just know there will be fresh butterbeans and tomatoes still warm from the garden when you pay your respects.

Ghoulish, you say? Not at all. That's how Pearlie would've wanted it. At least I think it is.

If you're not going home to funeralize, you're probably visiting the nursing home.

The last time I visited my husband's aunt at the Shady Havens Garden of Despair, I was a little late getting to her room because there was a sweet ol' thing pushing a walker standing at the entrance and screaming to anybody who came inside: *"Can't anybody in this place tell me how I can get saved?"*

My aunt-in-law's roommate was a pistol. Auntie shooed her away as she came over and foraged for one of the Payday bars she knew Auntie stashed in her bedside table.

"I can't keep a decent candy bar in this place," she hissed.

I was a little embarrassed by Auntie's outspokenness but I didn't need to be.

"She's deaf as a post," said Auntie. "Can't hear a thing."

But that didn't stop her from trying.

While I told Auntie about my only child's first trip to the bowling alley at age five, the roommate perked up.

"Is that Carmine Bowling, the one who used to run the Wash-a-teria?"

"No, no." I shook my head. "I said I took my daughter *to the bowling alley.*"

Roomie smiled widely.

"Yes, he was an alley cat, that Carmine. I think he was from up North, that's kind of an I-talian name. He may have been from Raleigh."

Auntie looked as if she wanted to scream but simply reached into her nightstand drawer, extracted a Payday, and started chewing, her dentures snapping like casta-nets.

Roomie decided this was a good time to hold court on all things Yankee.

"They tip for everything," she said. "You probably know that since you know Carmine so well."

Auntie rolled her eyes and made elaborate circles in the air beside her temple.

I had to agree with some of what Roomie was saying. Ever since so many Yankees have moved down South, everybody has his hand out, even the movie usher whose sole duty is to mumble "third theater on the right."

Like every former waitress, I tell Roomie, I am a generous tipper, but the proliferation of tip jars is starting to piss me off.

Frankly, after I've paid over three bucks for a small coffee, I'm thinking the tip is probably included. It's not like counter boy is Juan Valdez out there tying up the donkey and hauling the beans in from the back room.

And, if I do tip the jar, I consider it kind of a waste if no one sees me do it. It's the age-old question: "If a tip falls in a jar and nobody saw it, did it really happen?"

The copy shop now has a tip jar on the counter to reward employees who do what they were hired to do. You know. *Make copies.*

Although I could tell Auntie just wished I'd stop encouraging her, I told Roomie that I'd seen a jar recently that contained a long-winded plea that ended with "the rent is due and things are getting pretty tight."

"I love fair night, too," Roomie said.

Right. Fair night.

"You know what the best part is?" Roomie asked. "The sideshows! I once got to see the World's Tiniest Woman and it was the truth. She was so little she could fit inside a teacup and her legs didn't even dangle off'n the sides!"

Auntie perked up a bit at the discussion of sideshows.

"Biggest ripoff I ever saw," she said, ripping into another Payday. "I paid extra to see the girl who was born with two bladders. She just stood there grinning at us. I mean, when you think about it, it's not like you could really tell."

We agreed that, next time the fair was in town, we'd visit, the three of us. I knew Auntie would eat too many deep-fried Snickers and Roomie would never be able to hear those Air Supply tunes they blast all over the fairgrounds, but it would be fun if they had the diving mules again.

"You're right!" screeched Roomie. "Those Yankees are driving fools! Make it dangerous for all of us, you know."

'Deed I do.

Part 2:
Kids

*Just Because They Don't Have Gills
Doesn't Mean They're Human*

1
CHUCK E. *Cheese's*

**Where a Kid Can Be a Kid While Mommie Gets
Hammered on Watered-Down Bud Light**

*H*aving a child at age forty meant that I managed
to get through my entire twenties and thirties
without setting foot in Chuck E. Cheese's, a kid won-
derland where the star is an oversized, bucktoothed rat.

But when Sophie had a birthday coming up, she
begged for her party to be at the giant rat's crib ("Where
a Kid Can Be a Real Pain"). Kids love Chuck E. They
practically hold up tiny Bic lighters to coax him out of
the kitchen and onto the stage, where he gyrates his fat
furry butt to happy songs that are best listened to
through a beer haze.

It cracks me up that this wholesome family joint
serves beer by the pitcher but then I think the idea is
that you'll get so 'faced you end up tacking on a couple
of extra hours to sober up. Meanwhile, your kid is pump-

ing tokens into the whack-a-mole with the flushed desperation of a SAS-shoe-wearing senior at the nickel slots in Atlantic City.

Of course, the silver lining here is that, for every token, you earn "tickets" that can be redeemed for a prize before you leave. I don't want to imply that this is a rip-off, but the last time we went, I calculated that we spent $44.89 for a hot pink curly drinking straw. Of course, that's because we only had 5,580 tickets. To actually get enough tickets to claim the foot-tall stuffed Chuck E. at the "prize redemption" counter, you'd have to physically move into the building and play stomp-the-spider and skee-ball until you were old enough to develop cataracts, erectile dysfunction, *and* an inexplicable fondness for aspic.

At Sophie's birthday party, the kids chanted *"Chuck E.! Chuck E.! Chuck E.!"* until his royal rodentness finally emerged waving both arms to the kids, Nixon style. Several of the little girls visibly swooned and I feared they would have to be revived with red pepper flakes, which are on every table to add flavor to the "pizza."

If only the parents shared the excitement. From the moment my daughter's party invitations went out, parent-friends had the same underwhelmed tone as they called to flatly recite "We wouldn't miss it." Down to the last one, they rallied with genuine cheer, saying "Well, at least there's beer!"

Oh, but not nearly enough.

Don't get me wrong. This place is a kid's dream: games, ball crawls, tubes to get stuck in (I'm convinced there are still a few toddlers stuck in there from the late '80s somewhere just waiting to be freed and find out whatever happened to Wham!).

There are sing-along videos, a stage show with giant dancing animals, "Hi-waiian" punch, the works. One of my daughter's friends surveyed the surroundings and somberly announced, "It just don't get no better'n this."

Oh, sure it do, if you're over eight, in which case you pretty much think if you hear Chuck's theme song one more time you'll start chewing your own body parts just so you can quietly disappear.

When we arrived for the big party, I saw the beautifully appointed table for twenty in the distance and smugly congratulated myself on letting the rat do the heavy lifting this year. It was magnificent: neon sparkly derby hats holding color-coordinated helium balloons, confetti, party whistles. Stunning!

Unfortunately, it wasn't our table.

No, no. Our daughter's table was the one next to it with a paper plate and cup at each place setting and no balloons. It looked as if Tiny Tim had booked a party on the same day as Bill Gates's kid.

"Oh! The mom brought all those things," explained the relentlessly perky party attendant when I asked why it looked as if we would be serving piping hot bowls of gruel at our table.

"Listen, toots," I growled at her. "March your skinny ass back there, round up eight dozen balloons, and start blowing. Get rat-face to help you." She scampered away with fear in her eyes.

Our table started taking shape but then I noticed the competition had *three* videographers setting up tripods and a cake with the birthday boy's likeness fashioned out of tinted sugars.

"Who does he think he is? A Kennedy?" I hissed to my husband, who just hung his head and stuffed our $7.99 disposable camera back in his pants pocket.

I was starting to feel major mom guilt. After all, we hadn't taken our kid to Disney World that summer only because I was put off by a news report that some of the costumed characters were suing the company laundry, which was, you guessed it, a Mickey Mouse operation. The employees said their poorly washed costumes had even given them body lice and scabies.

As I explained to my daughter, once you've heard that Snow White's crabby, the fantasy loses its luster. ("Some-daaaay my ointment will come.")

And now, no videographer, a pitiful-looking table, and a cake that would only feed twenty kids if it was sliced thin enough to see through.

Once again, I had flunked the Mommy Wars, a sort of

self-imposed and unspoken awfulness that we suffer, a sick something that shows up at the worst times. Like in church a few weeks ago, when a beaming little family stepped forward to have their kid baptized and the minister shared that the tot was wearing "a baptismal gown that was worn by her great-great grandmother." "What?" I huffed to my seatmate. "They couldn't afford a new one?"

I first noticed the Mommy Wars a couple of Halloweens ago. Halloween is a silly holiday that I used to ignore except for a last-grab bag of Tootsie Pops on the way home from work at 8:00 P.M.

All that changes with kids. Halloween is much bigger, for instance, than my sturdy favorite: Thanksgiving Day. Halloween is sexy with witches, black cats, bloody ghouls. Thanksgiving was, like my daughter's table at Chuck E. Cheese's, an obvious also-ran, a dollar-store "Barbee," the one that's supposed to be just like a real Barbie but whose legs always snap off before you can get her to the car.

(My idea? Combine the Halloween and Thanksgiving into a mid-November "Hallothanks Day" where everybody dresses up as pilgrims and goes door to door trick-or-treating for maize.)

The Mommy Wars kick into high gear at Halloween. My daughter was invited to seven Halloween parties last year. By the time we got to the last one, her Little Mermaid costume looked like it had taken a detour through the Chicken of the Sea factory.

Halloween, as I see it, is just another chance for the Stepford Moms to do the superior dance over those of us who are craft-impaired.

While they're dutifully cutting plastic milk cartons they've saved for a year into ghostly luminaria or making a chocolate graveyard cake with Milano cookie headstones, I'm wondering why the hell anybody would need to *buy* cobwebs.

Back in the day, Halloween meant that my sister and I would wear a sheet or a foil crown and traipse to the school carnival for an hour or two to admire the spaghetti "intestines" and grape "brains" at the eighth-graders' Spook House.

Today, the Supermoms who host a haunted-house party are so competitive that I wouldn't be surprised if the human head on a platter was, well, a human head on a platter.

The mom competition continues through Christmas, of course. My mom-friends and I have an unspoken, and completely unhealthy, contest for the Perfect Family Christmas Card Photo.

I'm still seething over last year's card from my friend who dressed her sons as wise men, she and her hubby as Mary and Joseph, and her newborn son, lying in a makeshift manger, as the Christ Child. The Christ Child!

It's not like he can ever be an elf after that.

If I were catty, I'd point out to her that it is doubtful that the Christ Child actually had enough money to wear Hanna Andersson swaddling clothes. I'd also be unable to resist speculating that this woman is so competitive she only conceived a fourth child so she could complete her long-dreamed-of Bethlehem diorama.

Although she may have gone too far with her baby Kyle/Jesus, I have to admit that the simple sitting-with-the-drunken-and-slightly-lecherous-mall-Santa card photo isn't enough anymore.

I'm really tired of the baby Santa suits, too. These are the same kids who were pumpkins at Halloween. I'll bet they grow up resentful and anorexic with an irrational fear of oversized produce.

Last year, the card competition seized me and I dressed my daughter as a holly-topped candy cane and stuck her on the beach. In the cold. At high tide.

I can still hear her screams in my sleep.

Before Sophie was born, most of the cards we received were oversized, unfeeling, painfully tasteful cards from other childless boomers or the insurance company. Makes me feel all warm and mushy inside just thinking about the prestamped-in-gold signatures.

Today, our refrigerator looks like the pediatrician's bulletin board, each friend's holiday photo more elaborate than the one before it.

The Mommy Wars have sealed it as far as I'm concerned: Next year, it's Dad as the Grinch and daughter as Cindy Lou Who, complete with a teacup Krazy-glued to her scalp.

Now there's another buck or two hundred in the therapy jar.

I was thinking about all this as I stood with my daughter, watching her blow out birthday candles that were poked haphazardly into the frosting instead of placed in heirloom sterling silver holders like freak boy's were over at the next table.

Maybe it was time to simply say no and jump off this silly, mad carousel of competition.

"Mommy." My daughter looked up at me with shining eyes while Chuck E. himself held her tiny hand in his enormous, and somewhat matted, paw. "Can we have a backyard party next year? With just cake and ice cream and pin the tail on the donkey? Nothing fancy, just me and five or six of my best friends?"

Oh, I'm sorry. That's not what she said. What she said was, "Where's my pony? That boy over there said he's getting a pony today. *I want my pony!*"

"I'm sorry, honey," I said a little too loud. "Only children who are *adopted* can get ponies for their birthday."

So sue me. Sometimes it's just more fun to be naughty than nice.

2

"AND WHAT DID *YOU* Have for Breakfast, Dear?"

Tell the Preschool Nazis You Had Waffles and Eggs 'Stead of Juicy Fruit and a Coke, Okay?

All these weeks, on the short drive to the preschool, I've dutifully unwrapped a Nutrigrain bar and tossed it into the backseat to my four-year-old. Sometimes, I'll even unwrap one for myself. Studies have shown that it's very important for families to eat together.

This was all fine until a couple of days ago when I learned that, during "circle time," my daughter's teacher likes to ask the children, "Now, what did you have for breakfast this morning? Remember, everyone, it *is* the most important meal of the day."

Well, shit.

I felt embarrassed, ashamed, unworthy. Who knows what propaganda the other kids are spreading? Are they reciting menus of fluffy omelettes, homemade jams and jellies, turkey bacon and hand-squeezed juices?

"Teacher always asks us what we had for breakfast," my daughter said casually, while popping a nutritious and fruit-juice-flavored SweetTart into her mouth.

I damn near drove off the road.

Okay, let's not panic here. I mean it's not like we haven't been down this road before. Of course, our road is strewn with cheeseburger wrappers and half-empty containers of nugget dipping sauces.

I'm used to fudging the truth with the granola moms at the playground. One time, when my kid opened her lunchbox to reveal a Lunchables, I got a look from a mom with hairy armpits who would have been no less horrified if she'd seen my kid pull out a baggie full of white powder and a small mirror.

She flung her monkey arms wide and grabbed her own munchkin lest he see the vile Lunchable and start craving "pizzas" made out of white crackers and "pepperoni-flavored" type product.

Yeah, I know the stuff is crap but some days we just don't have time to go get a nutritious meal at the drive-thru.

Besides, I get addled at the fast-food drive-thru, especially if I'm ordering for a bunch of people. You try to get the orders right but then they all start screaming stuff in your ear.

"No mayo!" "Make sure that bacon's well done!" "Wait!

Change that barbecue sandwich to a grilled chicken, but no honey mustard and get some pickles on the side so Buford Jr. can do that scary Mr. Pickle Eyes thing he does for the young'uns."

My voice gets louder with every change until I find myself screaming stuff into the speaker like "Okay, forget all that! Buford Jr. wants a burger, no ketchup, and some tater tots."

Here's a tip: They don't know who Buford Jr. is.

Usually I just give up, burst into tears from the pressure, and settle on a big orange drink and a box of cookies.

Even if I get the orders right, there's that awful question looming.

"Would you like to make that a combo?"

Well, heck, yeah. I guess. I mean, should I? What do you think?

While others sizzle in line behind me, I'm weighing the benefits of upsizing against the guilt of starving children in sub-Saharan Africa in case I can't finish it all. If they ask if I want the two-for-one peach turnover special, we could all be there for days.

Back at the playground, the hairy mom was making quite the show of producing bagfuls of fresh grapes, which I have seen before in stores but never knew people actually bought. Monkey girl loudly mentioned that she was baking her own bread these days because of studies that showed many commercial bakeries had rat doo in their mixing machines.

While her bird-legged kid sat miserably munching a bag of dehydrated green peas from the hell food store, I popped a can of Pringle's like it was Champagne.

The moms I could handle, but teachers? That's something else altogether. Teachers have always intimidated me. When I arrive for parent-teacher conferences, I spend the whole time shifting from foot to foot, twirling my hair, staring at the floor tiles, and mumbling "yes, ma'am" to women fifteen years younger.

"Honey," I said, finally, "what did you tell the teacher when she asked about your breakfast?"

There was a deadly pause.

"I told her the truth," she said simply.

"Well, who the hell told you to do *that*?" I shrieked.

"You did! You said to always tell the truth. Don't you renember?"

I take time to be charmed for a nanosecond by the cute way she always says "renember" but then I realize that she has betrayed me to the authorities. I am so busted.

"Hmmmm," I said, running through a thousand possibilities that might be more impressive than yesterday's one-fourth of a Powerpuff Girl waffle and roll of Lifesavers (again, a fruit derivative, am I right?).

"Why don't you tell the teacher that you had two

scrambled eggs, a bowl of real oatmeal—the kind you have to cook on top of the, uh, you know, stove—two slices of whole wheat toast and a glass of soy milk?"

My kid laughed so hard a SweetTart flew out of her nose.

"Mommy, we don't eat like that," she said, howling.

Suddenly, I recalled a fascinating documentary on the morbidly obese I had seen on TV recently.

"No, but we should," I said with actual conviction. "And, starting tomorrow, or maybe the day after because tomorrow's going to be really busy, we will."

She'll have to help me renember, though.

3

"SORRY I CAN'T MAKE IT *to the Recital*"

I'm Planning to Poke Myself in the Eye with a Sharp Stick That Night

Unless you want your kid to spend the whole summer drooling into his Xbox and scratching his naughties, you better have a plan for keeping the lil punkin busy.

Having grown up in the country—yes, so far out that you had to ride a pregnant mule to the mailbox just to make sure you'd have a ride back home—I didn't know much about summer camps so it was a bit of a shock when I realized all my mom-friends were sending their daughters to ballet camp.

Some of these kids were still pooping in their pants but this didn't seem to matter to the moms. They acted as if three-year-olds taking ballet was as normal as executions in Texas and, Lord knows, I didn't want Sophie missing out on what one assured me would be "just the most important cultural opportunity of her whole, entire life is all."

I'm a little lazy about these things so I just signed up the princess where all her friends were going and where, I was assured, they didn't dress 'em up like little ladies of the night in those French ho can-can outfits.

I made the teacher solemnly swanee that, come recital time, Soph wouldn't be looking all Jon-Benet with a sequined bra, big hair, and Maybelline. That stuff just creeps me out, along with those hideous kid pageants where three-year-old boys wearing mullets and miniature tuxedos compete for Wee Master Southern States Universe.

To tell the truth, the ballet school "directress" sniffed at my makeup worries and said they had a strict no-makeup policy and she casually mentioned that the recital wouldn't last longer than thirty minutes *total*. She proceeded to yammer on about how the staff was full of ballet teachers with master's degrees in movement (who knew?) and how they were all trained at Juilliard and had been on Broadway or touring nationally for years and they'd all danced for kings and queens and presidents.

At the end of all that, I just stared at her in amazement. "You really mean it? The recital won't last more than thirty minutes?"

Toward the end of camp, we invited all of our closest relatives, friends, and neighbors to the recital. Guess what? Not a single one of them could come. Most said they had somewhere they had to be that day. When I pointed out that I hadn't told them the date yet, they said they had company coming or were planning some major surgery ("Which organ? Uh, I dunno. Heart, liver, brain, one of the big ones.") so the whole month was pretty much shot to hell.

I didn't blame them. I once went to a dance recital that lasted eight hours, no lie. You can only take a dozen or so five-year-olds tap-dancing to "The Good Ship Lollipop" before you're ready to dig up Shirley Temple and demand an explanation. What? She's still alive? Well, what*ever*.

At dance recitals, we get upset and outraged because everybody yaks until their own kid is on the stage and then they get all haughty. Talkin' 'bout: "What is wrong with you, you mo-ron? America-Sue is up there dancing her precious heart out and you pick this time to tell everybody about how your redneck cousin who's too poor to own a house or a car tried to kill his self by running his moped inside his tent with the flaps down. *I mean, do you mind?*"

I dropped my daughter off at her first day of ballet camp, grateful that a neighbor had given her a pink leotard, tights, and ballet shoes for her birthday. Being clueless, I'd just assumed they ran around in Pooh T-shirts and light-up sneakers for the first few years.

At the end of the first day, she ran toward me, clutching a picture of a ballerina that she had colored completely in red, face and all. Was this repressed rage or was her hair scrunchie just too tight? While I fretted about this, Soph reported that they "sangded songs," "playeded games," and "danceded some."

I likeded the sound of that.

Still, ballet wasn't enough to fill up a summer and that's where T-ball came in.

Having had zero success in organized sports myself, I was naturally apprehensive.

T-ball? On a team? With uniforms?

As it turned out, the princess was old enough, by just one day, to sign up. We considered this a good omen.

The first practice was an eye-opener. When the coach told his team to run a couple of laps, Soph said she didn't feel like running. I kneeled at eye-level, my voice a mommy-mix of calm authority and blubbery begging as I pictured the money spent on a bat, balls, glove, and sign-up fees disappearing faster than a Chilly Willy on a hot sidewalk.

When I pointed out that every other member of the team was running laps, she asked me if every one of them ran off the side of a cliff, should she do that, too. I don't know where she gets this crap.

"Just remember," I hollered when she finally took the field, "there is no 'I' in team!" Lame, but it's the only coachy phrase I knew and her daddy was still at work.

Just before her turn at bat, she balked at wearing the required batting helmet.

"Hell-o," she said to the coach, sounding like a size 6X Valley girl. "Someone else has worn this before?" She finally relented but only after we called for a delay of game so I could make her ponytail poke out of the back attractively.

It didn't take long to see that our team would need some work. In the outfield, they looked up at passing airplanes, down at blades of grass, basically anywhere but at the batter. One little boy spent the whole game practicing his running style. "Here I am as Peter Pan!" he shouted to his father, who promptly buried his face in his hands.

When a ball rolled past Soph, she eyed it without moving, then returned to digging a very deep hole behind the pitcher with the toe of her shoe.

T-ball isn't the big leagues. In professional baseball, you hardly ever see the second baseman burst into tears over a passing bee or a runner getting tagged out because she paused just short of first base to sing, "Who built the ark? No-ah, No-ah!"

Our team improved dramatically after a couple of brothers who looked way older than the age seven cutoff mysteriously signed up. One of them, I swore, had a pencil-thin mustache.

We won the first game according to my husband, who was actually keeping score.

"It's just for fun," I chided him, hefting my lawn chair into the trunk.

"We're not here to have fun," he said. "We're here to win. If we win, we will have had fun."

And from the backseat: "Daddy, how did my ponytail look when you were doing the video?"

The whole ballet-T-ball summer swirl made me realize that there's a lot of money to be made in kids' camps.

From the long list of camps offered in our town, it's obvious that anybody who isn't a registered sex offender can offer one. All you need is some skill, any skill, a few fliers, and some Sam's Club graham crackers. Once you got that, just sit back and watch the $145 camp fees roll in.

I'm tired of being the check-writer instead of the, er, writee. Think about it. The average camp has fifteen kids. That's $145 per kid times fifteen kids, which brings us to a total of, er, carry the two, uh. Well, lucky for you I'm not teaching Math Camp, isn't it?

Of course, the first step is deciding what skill you can teach a bunch of three-to-ten-year-olds. For me, that was the easy part. Next summer, I will teach a camp in Sarcasm.

Parents, by the end of the first morning, your child will advance from the tired world of "as if" and (shudder) "Not!"

You may think $145 is a little steep for a camp that doesn't so much as offer a chance to beat an African drum or fire actual clay into shapes resembling fresh dog poo, but, hey, you're paying for expertise here, not a bunch of silly supplies.

You say you don't think sarcasm is a virtue? Okay, I hear you. Just don't come crying to me if your kid gets his butt metaphorically kicked by one of the proud graduates of my Sarcasm Academy.

You probably have much more important things to attend to, anyway. I heard there was a big square dance and chicken bog extravaganza at the trailer park this week.

While teaching your children, I will draw on wisdom from the heavyweights of sarcasm such as *Friends* character Chandler Bing ("Could this summer camp *be* any more lame?").

Remember: Like most summer camps, I'll accept early deposits—cash only, please. If your summer plans change at the last minute, your money will be promptly and cheerfully refunded.

Oh yeah. *That'll* happen.

4

"YOUR KID'S FEVER IS SO HIGH, THE OTHERS ARE
Standing Around Her with Marshmallows on Sticks"

How My Day at the Spa Went Up Shit Creek

*L*ast *August* marked my four-year-old's first foray into formal education, where, presumably, she would learn how to use words like *foray*. At first, the preschool experience provided loads of "me time." While my daughter attentively studied one letter per week, I finally had time to get my roots done and eat lunch with friends in the kind of restaurants where there's no changing table in the restroom, foods ending in the word *fingers*, or a menu that can also be worn as a hat.

My newfound freedom was short-lived because by week eight (the week of *H* as in "hacking cough") Sophie had already had two colds, a stomach virus, an ear infection, and a mysterious rash. The Doogie working at the local "urgent" clinic—urgent being somewhat optimistic as we spent two and a half hours with the only reading material a breast self-exam pamphlet, which some funster had added nipple hair to—said the rash was "kinda gross." We left before he could proclaim my daughter's sore throat "gnarly."

Out the door and prescriptions in hand, I shook my head sadly and realized that I could've been a great doctor, much better than Doogie. I had always planned to attend medical school but there was just one thing I couldn't get past. I could not do ass work.

Every time I thought about helping and healing the sick, I felt a surge of pleasure until I reminded myself that there would inevitably be ass work.

Driving out of the clinic's parking lot, I wondered, for the bazillioneth time why I couldn't have just specified "no ass work" on my med school application if things had gotten that far.

The truth is, preschool diseases—all diseases—fascinate me. I've watched enough medical shows on The Learning Channel to easily pass the boards in a number of subspecialties.

Heart, lung, brain stuff, I would've been terrific, no doubt. But anything below the navel, well . . .

"You'll need someone else if you want to show me your ass," I would say, looking compassionate but firm in my starched white lab coat and serious-but-hip doctor glasses.

I know what you're thinking: why not psychiatry or

dermatology? Well, dermatology still offered the threat of a stubborn pimple on the ass. Unless, I could have opened a "Just Faces!" practice, like those vets who only do cats and small birds.

As for psychiatry, there's probably no ass work per se but you have a bunch of whiny asses coming in all day long. Nope, too close to the metaphorical rectal region for comfort.

I have tremendous respect for those who do ass work. What bravery to hang one's shingle out proclaiming "Practice restricted to diseases of the head, foot, throat, and ass."

As we headed into the drugstore to fill Doog's prescription, I wondered just how much this was going to set me back. The big pharmaceutical companies are reporting record profits while drug-poor seniors pop tops on Fancy Feast every night for supper. What do they *do* with all that money? They say it's all about R&D, research and development, that is, which is not to be confused with R&B or B&D, both of which are infinitely more fun.

I also remembered early warnings from friends who said that preschool would set us up for all sorts of contagious ailments that would lay the kids out like tiny Old Navy–clad dominoes.

One mom told me that a mean strain of an intestinal bug was making the rounds, apparently spread by kids who didn't wash their hands after making doody. She said it just like that, "making doody." She's forty-two and flies her own airplane. God help us all.

Because this bug could keep kids home for a week or more, I decided to spy on my daughter's classmates to make sure they were washing their nasty little mitts with soap and warm water.

Sure, the staff asked me to vacate the premises after the first three weeks but I must tell you that my research revealed that you should probably never hold hands with little boys whose first initial is *Tyler*.

Back at the drugstore, the line was long. Everybody was sick, it seemed. It reminded me of the lines at the grocery store last year when all the docs ran out of flu shots, but, strangely, you could still get one at the Piggly Wiggly.

I still haven't gotten past the whole grocery-store-as-health-care-center trend. I don't want to have a glaucoma screening, blood pressure, or diabetes check at the supermarket. What's next? Pap smears beside the succotash? Cardiac catheterizations sharing an aisle with the canned sausage?

After another half hour or so, we got the prescriptions filled and Sophie managed to make it to the letter *M* week without another ailment. But then . . .

Let's just say it: There should be a reserved seat in hell—where *Thomas the Tank Engine* starring Peter

Fonda in the worst children's movie of all time plays on all sixteen screens at Satan's Sin-a-plex—for parents who bring a kid with a 102-degree fever to school. ("What? She looks pale and clammy to you? Oh, she gets that from her father. Toodles!")

Don't they know they'll be summoned back to school by the stern voice of the principal on the answering machine? ("Could you please pick up Tonya Sue? Her fever's so high, the other kids are standing around her with marshmallows on sticks.")

Meanwhile, every kid at school is incubating the latest butt-kickin' virus and spreading it to the grown-ups at home.

The way I see it, thanks to some inconsiderate hussy who didn't want to cancel her French pedicure, I have wicked pinkeye and sound as if I'm going to cough up a Passat. Wagon.

My daughter announced during Q week that her friend had missed three days of school because she had "the Romeo."

It took some digging to discover that what she meant was pneumonia. Frankly, I liked Romeo much better and intend to use it if I ever feel my lungs rapidly filling with fluid. ("C'mon, Doc, don't sugarcoat it; you and I both know I've got the Romeo.")

It's funny how when you try to correct kids, they can get downright belligerent considering that you basically control 100 percent of the Ring-Pop distribution in the household.

"It's pneumonia, honey," I said.

(Loudly) "No, Mommy, you must mean Ru-monia." And, then, apparently in full preschool teacher mode, she added: "Now, watch my face and say it after me, ru-moan-ee-ya."

To which I just sighed deeply, suddenly very sad to have finished my wine, and dutifully recited "Rumonia." Which can also be spelled Uncle.

Some parents have told me that, practically speaking, it's actually a good thing to get these diseases out of the way now so the kids will be immune to them by the time they start Real School. That makes sense. I think I'll just crash my car to make sure the airbags are working, too. Who are these *M*-is-for-mo-rons?

Of course alphabets and diseases aren't the only things you learn at preschool. Last week, my daughter shocked me by asking for help settling a playground debate: did babies come out of your belly button or from Nordstrom's?

Sex talk? At four? Oh, holy hell. I hadn't planned this for at least eight more years.

Hadn't I done the best I could do? Didn't I yank *Legally Blonde* out of the VCR mere seconds after my daughter asked me softly, "Mommy, what's a bastard?"

I launched a rambling ten-minute, age-appropriate discussion about how babies are a gift from heaven. So sue me. The exact details can come later, on the school bus or under the bleachers, where every kid learns them.

If the Romeo doesn't get 'em, that is.

5

PRESCHOOL
Already?

**Why We'd Rather Stay Home, Chew Gum, and Not
Share a Little Longer**

We didn't send our three-year-old to preschool.
Don't get me wrong. Signing her up was on my
to-do list, along with picking up the Clinique bonus gift
with purchase, but I never got around to either of them.
My bad.

All of Sophie's little friends, who had well-organized
and clearly superior mommies, went to preschool, but I
wasn't all that impressed. Frankly, I figured my kid could
color at home and I'm proud to tell you that, by staying
home, she never missed a single episode of educational
programming such as *Dora the Explorer* or *Judge Mills
Lane*.

The funny thing was that every time I told somebody
Sophie wasn't in preschool, they would smile knowingly,

and say, "Ohhh, you're planning on home schooling her, aren't you?"

At this point, I laughed so hard I busted a couple of ribs and paramedics were summoned.

Don't get me wrong. Home schooling is fine for some folks. Maybe they're concerned about school violence or declining morals. Maybe they believe their kid can learn better in a nurturing environment that stresses individual strengths and creative learning approaches. Or maybe they just hate having to miss the second half of *Passions* to shlep to the bus stop EVERY FRIKKIN' DAY.

Home schooling? No way. I believe that education, like brain surgery and sausage making, is something best left to the professionals.

It's not that I didn't think about preschool when my daughter was turning three. I even visited a couple of them. One didn't smell like poop and every little room had an aquarium with a hermit crab to torture. But then I heard about The Rules.

Parents had to provide the snacks and there was a looong list of "unacceptable foodstuffs" which basically included every single item in my pantry. Peanut butter was out because of possible peanut allergies. Grapes couldn't be larger than your pinkie toenail. The whole thing made my head hurt.

Another preschool was just entirely too expensive at

$6,000 a year. Plus, parents were responsible for laundering the art smocks every week. I'm thinking for that kind of money they should come to my house and hand wash my step-ins, am I right?

I had several friends who sent their kids to preschool with such rigid parking rules that if you parked incorrectly they actually called your grown-up self into the teacher's office. My friend, Lisa, an ultra-competent mommy and big-shot corporate lawyer, was reduced to tears for a parking offense. I knew I'd never fit in. Somehow, the teacher would miraculously locate my old "permanent record" and would be only too eager to add a few negative comments. ("Forty years later, she remains a troublemaker who doesn't apply herself. Sigh.")

When Sophie turned four, the preschool pressure was too much and, frankly, I started looking at those nine hours a week when she'd be learning awful playground words like "bah-gina" (it's taken me weeks to convince her that the medical term for "down there" is actually "woo-woo") as a minivacation on the order of a trip to Bali, lounging in the sun, my every need attended to by a dutiful and buff cabana boy.

In our minds, it was already time to start thinking about Big School. It seemed like only yesterday that they had placed that tiny pink bundle into my arms and I was overwhelmed with awe and wonder. At least, I think I was. Hell, I was on so much Percocet, it may as well have been a squirrel monkey they placed in my arms but I'm pretty sure it was a baby.

Kindergarten? Already? My husband and I began to slowly and carefully freak out.

We're a teacher's worst nightmare. You don't believe it? Consider that we spent several nights visiting kindergarten open houses and *we carried clipboards*.

So what? So this. We did this one year early.

Several teachers scrambled for their roll books and looked puzzled when we introduced ourselves.

"There must be some mistake," they'd say. "We don't seem to have your daughter's name on our list."

"Oh no," we said. "No mistake. See, we are auditioning you. The princess is our only child and, frankly, we're not getting any younger, as I'm sure you've noticed, so we want to make sure that she has the best elementary learning environment since we'll be basically nodding off into our rice pudding at the home by the time she gets to junior high."

"I see," they said, not seeing at all.

"Hmmmm," I said, "don't you think these cubbies over here would be more attractive if you painted them in eggplant or sage so scuff marks wouldn't show?"

"Uhhhhh—"

"Speak up! I can't *hear* you!"

"*Uhhhhhhh—*"

"And this nest-building fighting fish over here," I said,

"he looks a little depressed to me. Have you considered letting him swim in a wide-mouthed vase filled with indigenous stones from North Carolina's ruby mines? Here. I brought a bag just in case . . ."

"Yes, well, thank you . . ."

Sophie, rolling her eyes and doing an "Oh, Mommmm" that I hadn't scheduled until puberty, scampered away to check out a *Pooh* program on the teacher's laptop.

"Will all the children have a computer?" I asked.

"Certainly," said one fresh-faced teacher who had developed a strange tic and was ma'aming me way too much. "We have three computers in each classroom for the children."

"So that leaves you about nineteen short. Let's work on that, shall we?"

"Well, it's not that simple," huffed an older teacher with eyeglasses on a chain. "There are budgetary considerations. We're doing the best we can with limited resources and dwindling public support."

"Oh, cry me a river," I said. "You've got a whole year to fix this. That is"—and, here I paused for effect—"if we decide to come here."

"Well, you know the plumbing's awful in this school," one teacher blurted out.

"Yes!" said another. "We haven't had a decent flush here since 1998. And don't get me started on the playground equipment. It's so rusty we have our own tetanus ward."

The whole experience was so traumatic, we decided to wait a year until we did, so to speak, have a dog in the fight.

Take it from me, hons. Selecting the right kindergarten is every bit as stressful as growing out your bangs. Foolishly, I timed these two life-altering events to take place in the same month.

When it finally came time to select a school, I was majorly stressed and it didn't help that my bangs were in that maddening fall-in-your-face stage that looks so terrific on Helen Hunt but made me look like I was working undercover as a dying fern.

As the sign-up time began in earnest, we mommies began to wonder . . . Public? Private? Charter? Church? Technology, foreign language, or arts focus? Inquiry-based or traditional? Year-round or nine-months' calendar? Magnet or neighborhood? Thin or hand-tossed?

We gathered in tight little circles on the freezing playground, scrutinizing test scores and ignoring our children's screams for help on the monkey bars. Sure they sounded terrified and their faces were tear streaked, but, hey, we're planning their futures here. A little help?

My sister, who doesn't have any kids, said she didn't get all the fuss as she heard me console yet another mommy-friend whose kid didn't get in the private school where, she sniffled, "all the kids' art looks just like Vincent van Gogh did it his own self."

I heard it was a good school but knew we wouldn't fit in. The teachers still wear Earth shoes and the parents have those annoying Kill Your Television bumper stickers on their perfectly aged Volvo station wagons. Losers.

"What's the big deal?" my sister asked. "Don't you just send your kids to the school closest to your house?"

I started with a review of inquiry-based learning and her eyes slammed shut and she began to snore loudly.

I couldn't blame her. To someone who was neither dealing with kindergarten issues nor growing out her bangs, the whole thing must have seemed so shallow and self-absorbed.

I mean, planes were being flown into buildings; we were a nation at war, for heaven's sake.

As it turned out, we chose public kindergarten at a magnet school so all that was left to worry about was my bangs. Oh, and that whole axis of evil thingy.

6

"PSSST—WANNA BUY SOME
Really Ugly Gift Wrap?"

Training Tykes to Be Telemarketers for Fun and Profit

*L*ast week I spied a brightly colored chores chart on my friend Lola's refrigerator, complete with thumb-sized magnetic cookies indicating that her four-year-old had made the bed, fed the goldfish, placed plastic juice bottles in the recyclables, and so forth.

Because our kids are the same age, I felt inspired to go home that very minute and create my own colorful laminated chores chart with headings including mow grass, replace rotted wood around dormers, take down storm windows and install screens, and so forth. I know what you're thinking but we don't have a goldfish.

This was going to be fabulous. Clearly the days of me running around like Edith Bunker fetching beers for Archie every time my daughter demanded more rainbow vanilla wafers were over.

The next morning, I told the princess that she would be starting her new chore life by making her bed.

"But you do that, don't you?" she asked, clearly horrified.

"Sure, I always have, but you're old enough to do it yourself," I said. "It says so in all the parenting magazines. Besides, I've made this nifty chart and you get a *dollar* if you do all your chores all week."

The princess rolled her eyes and went back to sleep. Maybe this had all been a bad dream. I imagined her dreaming of Norma Rae, standing atop her shut-down loom and demanding a wage increase or, at least, more E.T. Teddy Grahams.

Who was I kidding? This was the same kid who required that I ask her to put her shoes on approximately seventy-three times. No, really. The other day it suddenly occurred to me that I had been slowly repeating "Please put your shoes on" in a monotone for the better part of an hour like it was some sort of demented mommy mantra. I sounded just like those airport recordings: "The white zone is for the loading and unloading of passengers only. No parking."

Four-year-olds are selectively deaf, of course. They can hear the opening strains of *Spongebob Squarepants* if they're twenty-six miles from the closest TV, their little ears pointing toward the sound, their nose high, a paw slightly raised. Yet they cannot hear you say, *"It's time* to go. *We're going to be late,"* if you're kneeling with your hands on their shoulders and staring into their demonic little eyes.

I hear my boring self tell my daughter that when I was her age I was making my bed, feeding the oxen, and polishing my three-button shoes, but she doesn't hear a word I say.

Although now and again, she does ask me what the white zone is.

Ironically, while you'll have a terrible time getting kids to do chores around the house, it's amazing to see how quickly they accept the notion of going door to door selling crap for their school.

With all this pressure to be a good salesman, schools are churning out tiny little future telemarketers and I'm sure that we're all in agreement that that's exactly what this nation needs right now, more telemarketers.

Oh, but if your kid sells $500 worth of popcorn, candy, candied popcorn, wrapping paper, greeting cards, magazines, coupon books, chances on a used Taurus, he'll win a pink fur key chain shaped like a tooth that you know is worth precisely eighteen cents as well as the admiration and respect of the entire class.

They get the kids psyched up. *You must win the key chain.* And if you don't, you're stuck with a kid with Swiss cheese self-esteem. The kid's in prekindergarten but if he doesn't sell enough crap to win at least a little prize, he's already branded as lazy, a loser, *Not a Team Player*.

The parents at a neighborhood school got so into the fund-raising that they all made dresses and hats out of the wrapping paper they would be sending the kids out to sell. Don't any of y'all ever tell me I got too much time on my hands.

I've dreaded the moment that my daughter would be required to peddle junk door to door ever since I first found out I was, medically speaking, knocked up.

On the other hand, having bought enough of that junk from my newsroom co-workers back in my childless days, we were technically overdue. Now I'd be the annoying parent toting those damn boxes of foot-long chocolate bars their kids were supposed to be selling, the one who guilted friends, neighbors, relatives, and co-workers into buying one or six. Well. They are tasty.

Because we've already worked our 'hood for the Leukemia Society, Red Cross, and March of Dimes, my daughter and I are the poorly groomed version of the Jehovah's Witnesses. I've seen our neighbors run when they see us coming, screaming to their children to get inside just like the mosquito-spraying truck was coming down the street or something.

Yes, they dive to the floor and yank the curtains shut. We're like Moses and Addie Pray selling Bibles door-to-door in *Paper Moon*. Oh, except they were crooks. Then again, charging eight bucks for a three-pack of microwave popcorn could be considered stealing in some circles.

As I huffed down the sidewalk, a box of candy bars in each hand, I wondered again why we can't just write the school a check and get on with our lives. I mean it's not like this is a useful service. Most people don't hug us with relief, and say, "Oh, thank you!!!! Thank you!!! I was just telling my husband that I was so tired I dreaded going to the grocery store and buying our six oversized chocolate nougat bars for tonight. Oh, God bless you and your whole entire little family!!!!"

After it was all said and done, pink fur key chain in our possession, we basked in the strangely satisfying smiles from the homeroom teacher (one can only imagine that the kids who don't sell the quota are sent into the coal furnace to hang out with the pale and sweaty custodian whose personality reeked of Carl in *Sling Blade* and always called to mind the phrase, "Police described him as a drifter. . . .")

Although she was still having a devil of a time getting those storm windows installed, I decided it would be a good idea to take my daughter and her little friends for a well-deserved treat after all that Willie Loman–esque foolishness.

The children's museum was a surprise, honestly. I

thought it was going to be lifelike wax figures of Great Kids in History ("Kids, look! It's Danny Bonaduce from *The Partridge Family* when he was just a copper-haired cut-up instead of a burned-out DJ picking up transvestite prostitutes!") but it turned out to be a bunch of "hands-on" scientific experiments, animal facts, and art stuff. Talk about your bait and switch.

The tiny telemarketers in training were thrilled, although I wasn't. There was exactly one chair in the building for any weary adult who might have grown tired of oohing and aahing over the baking-soda-makes-volcano demonstration. Got it; it fizzes; let's move on.

I spied a muscular young dad holding a camcorder sitting on the only chair. Apparently, chairs, like Mesozoic Pterosauria, had become extinct. After a few minutes, he walked over and tied his kid's shoe. I leaped into the chair with the grace of the endangered dama gazelle.

Young dad turned back toward "his" chair, saw me happily sitting in it, and gave me the evil eye.

Now, I am no stranger to the evil eye but the guy had vacated the chair. Whatever happened to chivalry? He was at least twenty years younger than me and looked as if he could bench-press Indiana. He turned in a huff and perched illegally on a Lego sculpture that looked like it could pierce the, ahem, child-producing materials area if he so much as coughed.

The girls were happily playing, I had my chair, and there was a fascinating fight brewing between a six-year-old and her mom beside me. Suh-weet!

The kid was flinging a fit to be carried to her car. Her mother, one of those slim, muscular granola moms wearing garden clogs, was trying to use reason.

"I imagine that right now you are feeling sad about leaving and I understand that emotion," said the mom. She then proceeded to devise clever and fun-sounding ways that her daughter could go to the car.

"Perhaps you'd like to skip or hop on one foot all the way to the car!" she said brightly.

Whoa. What was this woman *on*?

Did she miss the whole parenting-by-bribery hormone that the rest of us got in the delivery room? The one that empowers us to say things like, "Junior, you either get your scrawny butt off that floor right now or you can just kiss your banana Popsicles good-bye and don't even *think* about that *Star Track* lunch box. (Rednecks always say *Star TRACK*, you know.)

I'm not saying that PBB is right, but I am saying it works.

In the end, the kid won, of course, and Mommie Weirdest hefted the smug and smiling sixty-pounder onto her narrow shoulders and carried her to the car.

I bet I know who sold all the candy in that family.

7

HOW TO BE A HANDS-ON PARENT USING
Field Trips, Dead Butterflies, and Beefaroni

In an attempt to expose our five-year-old to as much flora and fauna as she could possibly stand before she started kindergarten, we visited an alligator theme park, the state zoo, an aquarium, and a butterfly "pavilion," all in one week. And, yes, as a matter of fact, we are clinically insane.

First stop: the butterfly place, where there's also a bird room. Unlike normal zoos, where birds fly about in tall cages like God intended, this was an "open aviary" so you felt very much like Tippi Hedren in *The Birds* except without the safety of a telephone booth.

Four shrieking cocka-somethings landed on my husband's shoulders at one time and he damn near fainted. Our daughter began to wail when I screamed to him, "Cover your eyeballs!"

In the butterfly room, things were much calmer. Too calm, in fact. A soothing butterfly "counselor" explained how to lure a butterfly onto our outstretched honey-soaked arms. After an hour of wandering around, gooey arms stuck straight out in front, *Night of the Living Dead* style, we had not so much as a candle moth to show for our efforts.

"They hate us," my husband moaned. He was right. Multipierced teens and Reebok-ed seniors sat eating rain-forest crunch bars while enormous blue-and-orange butterflies nibbled their ears and nuzzled their necks. After ninety minutes, we were crazy with envy. We had painted on so much honey that we looked like walking baklava.

Finally, in a very low moment, I whispered to my husband, "You know, butterflies look pretty much the same dead as they do alive when they're not moving." Well, it's true you know.

At long last, hubby coaxed one rather puny brown butterfly onto his hand and so did our daughter. Two hours in, and all I had to show for our Fun Family Day was a smattering of bird poo in my hair from an enraged parakeet.

"We're not leaving till I get a !@#$% butterfly to land on me," I said, loud enough to earn a mean look from one of The Chosen, who was taking pictures of large lemon-colored butterflies gently flapping on the knees of her sleeping toddler.

"That is *so* not fair," I pouted. "That kid didn't even pay admission and I got fifteen ninety-five invested in this."

"Aren't those beautiful? They are called painted ladies," said a well-meaning woman wearing tan Easy Spirits and pointing to the orange wonders sweetly resting on her earlobes.

"Oh, shut up," I said with a bright smile.

"Relax," my husband said. "The butterflies can probably sense your tension."

Oh, great. He was suddenly Mr. Butterfly Expert just because he had managed to lure one substandard moth that was now helplessly mired in his honey-armhairs.

"See," my husband cooed. "He's not going anywhere! He's happy! Yes him is! He's a happy little butterfly."

You might wonder just what kind of depraved loser would consider a visit to a peaceable kingdom of butterflies a competition and, yoo-hoo, that would be me.

After three full hours, something did light on me, finally: the American Housefly, pestus grandus.

We decided to cut our losses, wash our arms off, and drive four hours to the zoo. I've always been a little afraid of zoos since I was five years old and my parents watched in horror as a lion peed on me through the bars of its cage during a family trip to Texas. I think somebody shot it. Things weren't so PC in those days.

But zoos are relentlessly educational. This would truly give the kid an edge in kindergarten. Besides, we'd read that it was the last chance to see Carlos the Gorilla because he would soon be shipped out to, get this, teach social skills to Atlanta gorillas.

Like every other North Carolina parent, I have met Carlos. And if you consider turning your hindquarters up in the air and into the horrified faces of your guests "good social skills," then, yes, Carlos is your man.

Having first met Carlos in the mortified company of my mother-in-law when my daughter was too young to remember him, I can't imagine why they think Carlos will be "something of an etiquette expert" when he hits Atlanta. As I recall, he had an inordinate fascination with his, er, Carlos parts.

We read that the North Carolina Zoo had spent quite some time preparing Carlos for the move to Atlanta and I envisioned that might include learning how to order various forms of chevre crostinis in trendy Buckhead nightspots. Turned out they just meant they had to train him, news reports said, "to enter a crate so he wouldn't have to be sedated during the drive to Atlanta."

What's wrong with a little sedation? This guy is thirty

years old, ugly as a mud fence daubed with tadpoles, and he wears the same stinky suit every day. I say give him as many drugs as he can stand.

Once safely ensconced in Zoo Atlanta's rain-forest exhibit, Carlos will show off his "etiquette training." One hopes this will include a demonstration of how to write a proper thank-you note.

WRONG: "Thanks for the bananas."

CORRECT: "Thank you for the bunch of bananas. We used them to entice the trainer to bake lovely banana-walnut-carrot muffins for Sunday brunch."

Of course, if he didn't like the gift so much, he could just turn his hindquarters in your face.

We were so eager to make sure that our daughter had a good start at her science and math magnet kindergarten (a phrase I can now actually say without snickering), that I even brought along some science books to read between our little field trips.

I chose them carefully because of all the flap about how many mistakes they've found in textbooks. The most hilarious of these boners was a photo of singer Linda Ronstadt that is captioned "Silicon Crystal," not to be confused with Ronstadt's songbird buddy, Silicon Crystal Gayle, I suppose.

As my daughter starts her formal education in public school, I have to admit that it's a little scary to find out that some of the textbooks are full of errors. Then again,

I feel completely exonerated regarding a certain eighth-grade experiment that went awry. (Note to Mr. Hodges: See, it's not my fault you still can't grow eyebrows.)

All the family field trips in the world won't help when kids are using books that—and I am not making this up—show the equator passing through the rural South or an incorrect depiction of what happens to light when it passes through a prism. Correct depiction: toss the light an orange jumpsuit and tell it to be very careful in the prism shower.

There was also a reversed photo of the Statue of Liberty showing the torch in the wrong hand, although I don't really see what that has to do with science anyway. Everybody knows from studying our history textbooks that the Statue of Liberty is actually a large piece of cheese first discovered by famous explorer Ponce de Leon Redbone and his ships, the *Larry*, the *Curly*, and the *Moe*.

Textbook researchers compiled more than five hundred pages of errors, then boiled them down to about one hundred, presumably because their heads were beginning to hurt. (And speaking of boiling, class, let us not forget that water reaches its boiling point at precisely two degrees Celsius or Fahrenheit, depending on whether the equator is setting in the west or the east that day.)

Despite these little problems, I was optimistic that,

after a frantic week of field trips, science experiments, and lunch-box buying, my daughter was finally ready for kindergarten.

We survived the first week pretty much as predicted. Day one: me sniffling, red-eyed, and videotaping ("Here she is placing her little Barbie lunch box on a little hook [sob] beside [sob] her little [sob] naaaame.") while my daughter rolled her eyes and said in a low voice, "Uh, Mom, don't you have somewhere you need to be?"

Harumph! Out of the mouths of five-year-olds. Clearly I couldn't compete with the new laptops, classroom iguana, and free cinnamon rolls. Hell, when I heard about the cinnamon rolls, I wanted to stay all day myself but feared I would hear that familiar refrain: *"Security!!!!"*

I'm not a typical kindergarten mom. While the others dutifully signed up for volunteer hours ("Bulletin boards are my specialty!" they wrote with little smiley faces), I just scrawled "No Crafts" in my best serial-killer handwriting.

On day two, my daughter wanted to take something for "share time" but she didn't actually tell me this until we were parked in front of the school that morning. Exasperated, I tossed her the loose gear shift knob and told her to share with the class that sometimes it takes Daddy forever to fix something *because apparently your needs come last!* All right, so that was probably unnecessary.

On day three, there was a curriculum meeting with all the other kindergarten parents. I arrived exactly two minutes late and found that the staff was already two minutes into the program. I'd totally forgotten how they take that punctual thing so seriously in school. Balancing my forty-five-year-old butt on a chair designed for a Cabbage Patch doll, I whispered to my seatmate, "I can't believe I'm missing *Fear Factor* for this." She gave me a don't-talk-to-me look.

On day four, I got a mean look from a skinny mom wearing a Greenpeace T-shirt and I knew she was cheesed because I was sitting in the carpool line, AC cranked up on high, reading a *People* magazine and eating God knows how much ozone. Oh, sue me. The carpool line is the most fabulous "me time" I've had in five years. You're doing something useful and important but you're all alone, icy air blasting, diet Coke in hand, and a terrific article about how much Brad Pitt likes mission-style furniture just waiting to be devoured. Life is good.

On day five, my daughter was in a particularly sunny mood because "We got two outside times and nobody even threw up." She explained that when somebody throws up or poops in their pants, the rest of the class gets to play outside. That seemed fair. We used to be the same way in my old newsroom. Her mood changed quickly, however, when she saw a new friend in the bus line. Suddenly, she was demanding to ride the bus like the other kids. Well, dookie. I love the carpool line. I had to nip this in the bud.

"I wanna ride the school bus!" she wailed.

"Fine," I huffed back. "You'll bounce all over town like popcorn and learn all kinds of new swear words."

"But that's just like riding with you, Mommy."

Ouch.

After a few more weeks of this, I decided that I should be a more involved kindergarten mom. If for no other reason, if I was more of a classroom mom, my kid might manage to stay out of the euphemistically named "thinking chair," where, I'm told, the little girl who likes to lick everyone's nose has to go for a few minutes every day.

Out of guilt, wistfulness, or maybe just because it's been a while since anybody offered to lick my nose, I signed up to shelve library books.

Three hours later, I was silently cussing the fact that they had given me all the 500s on the bottom shelf. My knee joints seized up and, for a panicky few minutes, I was positive I'd have to duck-walk out of the school and into the parking lot. ("Hmmm? Oh no, nothing's wrong. I just had to shelve some books today. Quack-quack.")

In a surge of motherly devotion, I even ate lunch at school one day.

"What is it?" I asked a third-grader as a ladle full of something tomatoish went splat onto my foam tray.

To paraphrase Andy Griffith, what it was was Beefaroni. And I must say it was shockingly tasty.

"See?" my daughter said in some psycho role reversal. "Sometimes you find out you like something if you'll just try it."

If you've never eaten with kindergarteners you don't know true popularity. As the only grown-up in our corner of the lunchroom, I was asked by no fewer than six kids to open cheese sticks, milk cartons, and fruit roll-ups. One rather spoiled little girl asked me to peel her grapes but I told her to wait until we got home.

At lunch, I nearly fell off my undersized molded plastic chair when I heard my daughter and her friend discuss where babies came from.

"Babies come from God," said my daughter.

"No, they don't," said her friend, shaking her head for emphasis. "They come from your bah-gina."

When all is said and done, hanging around school still isn't easy for someone who spent way too much time writing "I must nots" and washing blackboards. When I showed up to take my kid out of school an hour early, the assistant principal asked why.

Suddenly, I was thirteen again, lying to avoid the horror of having to wear that red one-piece gym suit in PE.

I mumbled something about how we'd be doing lots of higher math because we were going to the outlets. I even ma'amed her even though she's a good twenty years younger than me.

The truth is, I honestly like kindergarten, and not just for the Beefaroni. My favorite part? The communication via backpack thing. It's so efficient. Class pictures or T-shirts or announcements or report cards are sent home in the backpack; payment or comments or signatures are sent back the same way. Sort of like some wonderful Pony Express only with Powerpuff Girl saddlebags.

The whole thing makes me think that we should all communicate via backpack in this great nation using sweet little flower-shaped notes.

Bush to Saddam: "Do you like me? Check one, yes or no."

Don't thank me now. Just send me that Korbel Peace Prize.

Part 3:
COUPLES THERAPY,
Southern Style

Lord, Please Don't Let Me Kill Him
Till the House Is Paid For

1
"PAPA,
Don't Preach"

**You're Late for Church, Got Mary Kay on Half Your
Face, and He's Honking in the Carport**

*W*hy *is* it that Sunday morning, the time when you
should be enjoying a mood of gentle reflection
and contemplation as you get ready for church, is the
most stressed-out, irritating time of the week?

Sure, everybody ends up in the car and you, sort of,
make it on time (although my husband likes to say we
attend "the eight-forty-two service") but most of us are
still tugging on jackets and swatting Pop-Tart crumbs off
our pants when we arrive.

Typical is my friend Lee's childhood memory: "Daddy
would pace like a caged boar waiting for us to get ready
and get in the car. He'd pretend to read the paper but,
after a while, all you could hear was him snapping the
pages and sighing."

When he could stand it no longer, Lee's daddy would

noisily leap from his squeaky recliner and boom to an empty room: *"I'm starting the car!"* This was always greeted with groans. Lee's mother, after all, was still running around in her Shadowline slip with Mary Kay beauty-in-bisque on just the top half of her face like a carnival mask.

Lee's daddy would sit in the car, engine running, revving it ever so slightly until the whole family, grouchy and with shirttails hanging out, lurched down the steps and into the carport, slamming doors and jabbing elbows for the sullen Sunday ride to the house of the Lord.

It's not much different at our house. My husband, whose Sunday morning duties include dressing himself, memorizing the box scores, and fixing his own cereal, can't understand why it takes me so much longer to get ready. I dunno. Maybe it's because I must shower, get dressed, outfit the princess in her favorite "sunny school" dress complete with lacy socks and patent leather shoes, discover there's a gigantic rip in her favorite dress and explain why, no, she can't wear her Barbie nightgown with her church shoes, no matter how many sparklies it has in it. Then I must make her breakfast, fish my earrings out of the back of the toilet tank (don't ask), round up snacks and a change of clothes, inhale a burned toaster waffle, stuff a sack of canned goods for the food bank, well, you get the idea.

An elderly friend of mine said she remembers the time she and her husband groggily got themselves and their three preschoolers ready for church only to discover as they smugly situated themselves in the pew with a minute to spare, that, hmmmm, someone was missing.

They raced back home to find their two-year-old happily playing in the driveway mud.

I know it's not just us because every week we see at least two or three other families sitting in church, perfectly dressed with soaking wet hair.

And because, when the ushers pass the offering plate, the sound of checks being ripped out of checkbooks can drown out the choir. Once, I got so addled after we raced in late, I made the check out to Piggly Wiggly.

One of the reasons we are chronically late is that I teach Sunday school to second- and third-graders and, being a huge fan of working under pressure, I like to discover that I must "paint a Last Supper backdrop" the morning I actually have to show up with it. The night before church, I have stayed up late making all sorts of pathetic arks, mangers, and man-eating whales so by the time I show up for class I am too tired to do much except throw out some Ritz Bits and tell them to wake me up in forty-five minutes.

I would love teaching Sunday school except for the crafts part. For a long time, I tried to hide my secret: all the other moms were relentlessly competent, the kind of women who save Pringles canisters and paper towel tubes "just because."

One lesson had us making birdhouses out of tongue depressors dusted with glitter—apparently to attract Vegas-bound birds. Another had us using tongue depressors to construct Noah's ark picture frames. One wonders if doctors are able to get a hold of these things considering the insatiable craft community's demand. ("Sorry, Myra Jo, I can't see your tonsils today. Bobby Jr.'s building an ark.")

Church ladies are almost always crafty and I am convinced that heaven will be filled with their handiwork, including the woven-ribbon Bible bookmarks I can't make. Unlike the other church moms, I do not own my own monogrammed, double-action, chrome-handled glue gun. My daughter's first four-word sentence was uttered in the church fellowship hall after I glued my fingers together while trying to make a burning bush.

"Mommy can't do it," she said.

While I tried to unglue my fingers, I listened to the other church moms chat about crafts they'd been working on. There were bubbly descriptions of birthday cakes for sleep-overs that were shaped like a real sleeping bag; puffy hand-stitched memory quilts, handmade charm bracelets, and even talk of the dreaded Creative Memories scrapbook.

Many of my mom-friends have joined the Creative Memories cult and it has taken over their lives. Their families eat TV dinners while they spend hours using funny curvy scissors to cut pictures illustrating Junior's first everything. One friend said she became frantic when she realized she had failed to take a single picture of her son's first Fourth of July so she dressed him up in stars and stripes and put him outside the next January.

"Who's ever gonna know?" she asked, then laughed maniacally. The hair raised up on my arms.

I guess I knew the crafts thing was going to be a problem six years ago when my very first Sunday school teacher task was to "build an Easter diorama."

Say who?

This was not unlike "Define the universe; give two examples."

I had no idea what a diorama was, let alone how to build one. Over the years there have been plenty more scares (I still have trouble talking about the exploding baby Moses baskets in the microwave, although his head was still edible).

The one thing I have mastered is how to glue tissue paper to baby food jars so it looks like a stained-glass window. Okay, actually, it just looks like tissue paper on a baby-food jar, but have a little faith, would you?

As much as I enjoy church, even factoring in the early morning tension and glue gun fiascos, I admit to dreading the biannual church directory photo session.

Portrait day is always the one where you're late getting home from work, there's half a latte staining the front of your shirt, and your kids go from zero to pinkeye in the time it takes you to drive two miles to the church.

Because these photo sessions never run on time, you may have to pinch your toddler's thighs just enough to get her to yelp.

"Past her bedtime, you know," you mutter pathetically to the portrait counselor in a vain attempt to move your appointment up. When that doesn't work, you could try the ever-reliable: "They haven't ruled out cholera. . . ."

Because these are church portraits, there are never any of the nifty props that you'd find in a glamour-shots studio. I love those glamour-shots pictures and my favorite thing in all the world is when a dead person's family picks the glamour shot to use in the obituary.

It's like, you recognize the name but whoa! I never remember seeing Ethel Rae wear that jaunty sequined cowboy hat tilted just so. It's just so precious, that sweet old Southern face having the last laugh from under a pound of pancake makeup, boa snaking around her neck.

The last time we went for church pictures, we were finally ushered into the room where the photographer puts you on a little stool that puts your head even with your husband's shoulder. I used to be uncomfortable with that whole dominant-male image as my husband fairly towered over me in these pictures but now I'm just grateful to have something to lean on. Must be past eight o'clock by now. Decent people are asleep.

After it's over, you are shown to a little room where, thanks to the miracle of digital whizbangedness, you can actually *see* your pictures before you order them.

While you're thinking, "Hey, we don't look half bad," the portrait counselor, a graduate of many fine sensitivity-training seminars, mentions that for only forty bucks extra for airbrushing, no one will ever notice that you have what appears to be the beginnings of a goiter.

After this, she shows us a huge portrait of a particularly handsome family that has been turned into an actual oil painting for a few hundred dollars extra.

I agree that they look fabulous and ask to buy them on the spot.

"No, no, dear," says the counselor. "The portrait would be of *your* family; this is just a sample."

I knew that.

2

"NEVER SAW 'EM BEFORE *in My Life*"

What to Say at the Wedding Reception When Hubby's Dressed Your Kid in Batman Sweats and Tweety Bird Swim Socks

The toddler ahead of us in line was wearing a summery floral-print shirt, a striped skirt, mismatched socks, and shoes on the wrong feet. I looked at my friend and grinned. "Daddy dressed her," we said in unison.

Sure enough, she was standing with her daddy, mom nowhere in sight, probably working in an office somewhere, blissfully unaware that her husband had taken their child out in public wearing pink plastic sparkly sandals from the Dollar Tree.

Men think this is cute, even endearing. Women think that taking their child out in public looking tacky is grounds for divorce. ("Your Honor, he deliberately ignored the adorable Gymboree leggings and top I had laid out—not to mention the matching bow, embroidered socks, and coordinating fleece jacket—and he dressed Kayleigh Sue in her older brother's pajama top and the bottom half of a Jasmine costume. What? Jasmine, from *Aladdin*, Your Honor. Where have you *been* the past eight years?")

My friend, still observing the scene in line, sagely noted that "men never know how to put an outfit on their kids."

I pointed out that "outfit" is not a word in the male vocabulary. Men think it is good enough to get something, anything that remotely resembles clothing, on their child's body. If you ask daddy why little Sammie showed up at church wearing camouflage thermal underwear and a Power Ranger belt, he'll just say you're too uptight and, "it's just clothes."

And if their arms and legs fall off, I suppose it's "just leprosy."

My husband is as guilty as any of 'em. One night he was in charge of getting our toddler dressed for a Christmas party because I had to work and was going to join the two of them at the party.

He dressed her in a frilly red dress, so far so good, orange tights, and, Lord have mercy, white patent leather sandals.

I walked into the party and assessed the situation in a split second.

"Look," the hostess purred. "Your husband and daughter are already here. See, they're right over there by the fireplace."

"Who?" I snapped. "I never saw those two before in my life."

What else could I do?

A friend confided that she no longer allows her husband to dress their infant after she came home and discovered daddy had had trouble figuring out the whole footed-sleeper concept so he cut the feet out of all the baby's sleepers.

"I got pretty good at it, too," he had bragged. "Of course, the first one was hard because she was still wearing it. . . ."

Men don't stress about "little things" like whether socks match or hair is combed. In fact, men don't stress about much of anything, at least not the stuff that we think is important.

My friend Teensie called me last week, crying so hard I could barely make out what she was saying. A death in the family? Sickness? An accident? Had she lost her job?

When she finally calmed down enough to speak, I realized she was talking about her husband.

"I . . . had . . . every . . . week . . . and . . . he . . . just . . . *threw them away!*"

Teensie didn't need to say another word. I realized her husband had tossed out the loyal-shopper frequent-buyer coupons you get at our local grocery store chain.

See, if you shop ten out of twelve weeks and spend at least forty dollars, you can get free stuff. Good stuff like turkeys and towels and gas and even cash.

We have all become a little obsessed with this give-away coupon thing. Here was a woman who is getting her Ph.D. in Russian studies and she is sobbing hysterically because her husband trashed eight weeks' worth of Gobbler Dollars.

I felt her pain. Hadn't I choked on the Thanksgiving Giveaway last year? Sure, I had ten coupons, but they included three week sixes, a rookie mistake.

Listen to me. I don't care if you only have a jar of garlic olives in the refrigerator and the kids haven't had cereal since Saturday, you don't go to the grocery store until the next coupon week starts—always on Wednesday.

Last Monday, my husband began to whine about the lack of diet soda in the house.

"Are you *insane?*" I shrieked. "We can't have soda again until week seven. Do you have any idea how close we are to *free gas?*"

"But I'm really thirsty," he started.

"Then try *this!*" I said, wrenching the cold water faucet on. "It's called *water!* Get used to it!"

Those of us who are good at this coupon thing have little patience for those who aren't, or the people who tell the cashier rather high-handedly, "Oh, I'm not collecting those things."

Hmmph. Guess their cars run on snob juice.

This is the sort of stuff we women micromanage day in, day out, all week long. Men don't do this because it would take valuable time away from calculating the earned run average of some long-dead ballplayer.

Nothing fazes men. I couldn't help but notice the relaxed faces of the fathers at our neighborhood Easter egg hunt recently.

Their fingers and best khaki shorts were not dye stained; they looked refreshed and relaxed as they chatted against the deck rails, looking like a JCPenney casual menswear ad, only slightly less gay. I shouldn't have been surprised how happy they looked since the only real contribution a man makes to a party is to buy the ice.

A quick survey of my women friends reveals that, in most households, the man believes that once the ice is bought and the bags have been beaten on the deck (men love that part) and dumped into the cooler, it's party time! Invitations? Food? Crafts? Decorations? That stuff's for sissies, for people who say "cute and little" together.

No wonder these men looked so well rested. Meanwhile, their wives had fallen, exhausted and face-forward, into the bird's-nest cookies made out of melted chocolate and chow mein noodles that are a bigger pain in the ass than you'd think. The women had spent half the day filling and hiding 578 plastic eggs in the bushes, trees, transmissions.

You can tell how long a couple has been married by the degree of enthusiasm they can inject into the statement: "Biff? Oh, he got the ice!" The dewy-eyed newlywed can say this with the same awe with which she might announce that her husband had thrown himself on a live grenade to save a vanload of orphans.

Just wait a few years and you get the exaggerated eye roll and "Biff? Oh, he got the ice. He only got three bags because his back has been hurting ever since that football injury in high school. Yep, it's been twenty-six years but apparently when the team bus hit that pothole, he was never the same."

Perhaps it's as simple as admitting that getting the ice satisfies the much-ballyhooed hunter-gatherer instincts of primal man.

You don't really get that awesome surge of testosterone when you're hand-tinting several dozen bunnies-on-a-stick, do you? But the ice, the *ice!* Why, not only do you get the ice but you also get to pick up a copy of *Baseball Weekly* at the same time so you've managed to fulfill your duties *and* carve out a little me time.

Maybe it's our own fault. We women have a way of letting men know that, no matter the task, we can do it better. Even as my husband poured ice into the cooler recently, I fumed that he didn't put half in, layer the drinks, then another half on top.

"If you think you can do so much better," he bristled, "next time, *you* go get the ice!"

"Are you kidding?" I shrieked. "That's the one party chore you have left!"

"Don't worry," he said, an evil grin spreading across his face. "I'll get the kid dressed for the party while you're gone."

3

STUDY SAYS MEN LISTEN
with *Half Their Brains*

They Use the Other Half for Caulk

A new study offers medical proof of something we women have long suspected: men listen with only half their brains.

The fact is, if you're a man and you're reading this, there's a good chance you've already lost interest in this subject, dropped this book like it's a snake, and gone off to caulk something, anything.

The study by Indiana University's medical school found that men only use one side of their brains when they're listening and women use both sides.

To be fair, there's a school of thought (okay, half a school for men) that believes these findings simply mean that men are more efficient listeners, able to accomplish the same task while using half as much brain.

Then again, who wants to be fair?

I have long suspected that my husband, a man-type individual, hears only half of what I say during a typical conversation. Now I know it's not his fault.

Men apparently listen with just the left brain, which, as everyone knows, is associated with analytical thought, reason, logic, and the ability to urinate outdoors and not flap your hands and go "ooooh, icky!" afterward.

Most men have very little or no use for the right side of the brain, which contains information on family birthdays, anniversaries, Jenny K jewelry sale dates, and a delightful hodgepodge of zesty and nutritious casserole recipes.

This research certainly explains a lot.

Like how men and women act different on the Supreme Court.

Remember a while back when the high court was trying to decide whether Gore or Bush should be president?

The girl and boy justices handled the matter completely differently, if you'll recall.

The man justices would all interrupt each other and talk about golf scores and stuff while Justice Sandra ("Boom Boom") Day O'Connor thoughtfully considered the lawyers' arguments.

Consider this excerpt from a transcript of the high court's proceedings:

Justice Scalia: "Thank you very much, Counsel. Hey, has anybody seen my robe?"

Justice O'Connor: (sighing heavily) "It's right over there on the bench where you left it, Tony. I swear if your head wasn't attached to your shoulders . . ."

Justice Thomas: "What? What would happen if his head wasn't attached to his shoulders?"

Justice Souter: "You know, I'm getting kinda hungry. Let's just send this puppy back to the folks in Florida to decide, okay?"

Justice O'Connor: "Truthfully, I'm not sure that this was ever an intelligent exercise of appellate power—"

Justice Thomas: "Florida? Ahhh, Indian River fruit. Best stuff in the world. I don't even mind the seeds it's so good. Hey, one time I was in Florida and I got one of those little gift shop gizmos where you pour the whisky in the top of the little boy's head and you push a button on his backside and he pee-pees the whisky right into your glass. Man oh man, that was funny!"

Justice Scalia: "If my head wasn't attached, good one, uh, uh, Mandy."

Men don't have the capacity to talk like women do. Another study, this one by *Working Mother* magazine, reported that women discuss an average of forty topics when they get together for a typical night out, while men discuss just four.

Even with my regulation-issue girl math brain, I can cipher that to be ten times as many subjects discussed. Not that I'm shocked. Men have the whole conversation thing condensed to the final four: beer, sports, women, and work.

I decided to test the truth of this study during a recent night with some gal pals. Lisa, Michelle, Susan, and I have gotten together one night a month since we all attended pregnant aerobics class together back in '97. Lisa calls us PALs (pregnant aerobic ladies), which is cute and the exact kind of thing that a man would never, ever think of.

I started the conversation ball rolling by telling the absolutely true story reported to me by a friend who found herself in gastrointestinal hell after eating a bad fish taco. Turns out, not long after she ate the taco, she decided to drive over to her friend's house across town to return a very nice casserole dish she had borrowed for a dinner party.

As she was driving, her belly began to make horrible noises and she was in such distress, she pulled her mini-van over to the curb. As sweat beads popped on her forehead, she channeled the wisdom of her foremothers, looked around the van for a solution, and spied the casserole dish. She pounced on it, hiked up her cute little Talbot's jumper, and did a BM right there in the casserole dish.

After she was finished, she politely placed the glass lid on top of the dish, pulled over to the nearest Dumpster, and gently dropped her doody dish inside. Because this was in an inner-city area that was known for Dumpster diving at night, she said she nearly wept at the thought that somebody who was hungry and homeless might happen upon her doody casserole and get the shock of his life.

Because she was a good Southern girl, raised right, don'tchaknow, she wanted to write a little note on top saying Do Not Open but she didn't have a pen or paper and it wasn't the kind of neighborhood you wanted to hang around in.

That got things off to a great start, as you might imagine! The rest of the evening we discussed, in order: liposuction; what kind of a woman actually gives another woman a Brazilian wax, because you know you have to have your calves touching your ears for that thing; the new mayor's performance; a foolproof Caesar dressing recipe; at what age boys should stop wearing anything smocked (consensus: age three); how we knew Angelina and Billy Bob wouldn't last when they started wearing each other's blood round their necks, which just meant they were trying too hard and they'd end up shipping that poor Cambodian boy they adopted back like he was a busted barstool from Ikea.

This was followed by . . . facial hair; Afghanistan; facial hair in Afghanistan; how sistah-girls can get away with eating anything when they wear that sweaty-ass burkah so it's not all bad; how it's really awkward to see someone you know in the grocery store and then you have to think of something new to say to them when you keep meeting them on every aisle or else just pretend to really need something on the bottom shelf until they can go away.

Shoot, that's thirteen and the bread basket hasn't even arrived yet. We followed with: Enron; Ronnie Reagan; da-doo-ron-ron; how to pronounce Ilyanla's name and wonder if she signs her checks with a little exclamation point like on TV; speeding tickets; the comeback of fishnet pantyhose . . .

There was more of course: how pineapple salsa always gives me bad dreams; is brown or gray the new black; why nobody RSVPs for a kid's birthday party and how that makes you crazy; the trend of sending invitations to big-budget parties for engaged couples and then, on the same invitation, hitting you up to help pay for it (consensus: tacky beyond words); liposuction (well, it had been an hour); Russell Crowe; crow's feet; the Black Crowes (this is typical estrogen stream-of-consciousness stuff; try to hang); Chelsea's sleek new bob; Sarah Jessica Parker's sleek new bob; how we'd have kept the curls; the Winter Olympics; how somebody's brother-in-law used to live in Salt Lake City and said they do, too, drink coffee out there; how our waiter looks exactly like Joey on *Friends.*

That's close to forty and we haven't even seen the dessert menu yet. Face it, my hons: Girls rule. And we also never shut up.

4

BIG SCREEN, *Big Tallywacker*

Shoot, Everybody *Knows That*

The day my husband arrived home with a shiny big-screen TV, I finally understood male TV envy. But first things first.

"Can you give me a hand with this?" he asked.

Slipping into TV mode, I announced, "Survey says! I'd have an easier time trying to pry Louis Anderson's big butt out of the truck than unloading that thing."

"It's . . . not . . . as . . . heavy . . . as . . . it . . . looks," he huffed, tiny drops of blood spilling from his eye sockets as he pulled and tugged one corner of the box. It didn't budge. In fact, the TV seemed to shrink deeper into the depths of the truck as though it wondered what kind of nut house it was going to spend between ten and twelve years of fully warranteed service in.

I told my husband that I would "surely bust an ovary"

if I lifted anything that heavy. The mention of female parts sent him scurrying for man-type neighbors to help, just as I knew it would. Women have long realized that the mere mention of their "females" can get them out of just about anything, the notable exception being a very insensitive North Carolina highway patrolman who once refused to believe I was speeding because "my uterus told me to."

Moments later, my husband arrived with two burly neighbors who had interrupted their Saturday afternoon football watching to help out. There are certain things that men simply can't resist, with watching a game on a big screen or seeing Anna Kournikova eat a banana being at the tip-top of the list.

It did not escape me that it was going to take two WWF types to do what my husband had expected me to do.

There was a brief moment of panic after we all had some trouble locating the English instructions for hooking all the gizmos into each other. I don't know why there can't be an English-only manual available when you buy anything requiring assembly.

Is some weird political correctness run amok responsible for the fact that even your waffle iron comes with page after page of operating instructions ensuring that even Sanskrit devotees can enjoy a fluffy Belgian now and again? I bought a curling iron last week with operating instructions including every imaginable language, living and dead, including little hieroglyphics of what looked like a curly-haired deer leaping through a forest.

While the boys tore packaging apart looking for the English instructions, it occurred to me that it's less about being PC and more about economics. It would cost much more to print owners' manuals in different languages. So voilà! Bravo! Wunderbar! Hop Sing!

Maybe I hate plowing through all these languages because it's an in-your-face reminder that after three years of high school Spanish, the only thing I know how to say is "Oh no! I forgot my notebook!" or the equally useful "Hello. Can John and Mary come to the party at the public toilet?"

While the guys hunched over the (hallelujah!) English instructions, I recalled the Bookshelves That Nearly Ended My Marriage. The instructions were folded accordian style. Step 1 was right up front but steps 2–256 were scattered all over the place. I spent hours flapping and folding with my husband, finally giving up after the English instructions morphed into what appeared to be a rare Hopi Indian translation. Perhaps the Hopi, a proud people, share my fondness for cheaply made particleboard shelving. Perhaps not.

Once the TV was finally hooked up (the "little woman" got to clean up all the packing materials, natch), the guys sat down in reverent awe.

"That sure is a good picture," one said.

"And big, too," said the second.

"Yep. It's good *and* big," said my husband. "You know they threw in a DVD player with purchase."

"*Naw!!!!*" they howled in unison.

Then, and I knew this was coming: "How late you think they're open?"

While the football game raged in our small living room ("You can practically smell their sweat," my husband noted, choking back tears of happiness), the mood grew solemn.

"I only got a nineteen-incher, can you believe that?" one grumbled.

"Sure can," crowed my husband. "Until today, we just had a twenty-one."

Clearly we had moved up in the world, just as surely as the Jeffersons had achieved that "deeeeluxe apartment in the sky."

Since we got the big TV, our neighbors like to joke that they've canceled their premium cable because they can just watch our TV from across the street and read the actors' lips.

Har-dee-har-har.

During the day, I get to watch *Days of Our Lives* on our new humungous TV. As loyal as I am to *Days,* I can't say I was surprised to read recently that there has been a big decline in soap-opera viewing.

Let's face it. Soaps used to be downright educational. Where else would you learn about the sorrows so many of us face in our daily lives: extramarital affairs, alcoholism, child abuse, and, oh yes, the constant threat that an evil twin will resurface after twenty years on a remote Pacific island to take over our family and thriving medical practice?

The evil twin was about as wild and silly as it got back in the good ol' days of soapdumb. Not anymore.

Today there is real shame in admitting you still watch the soaps. Not too long ago, I asked some play-group moms if anyone had managed to catch *Days* and their looks told me that I was as uncool as *Dynasty* shoulder pads.

Okay. So soaps don't move very quickly. Yesterday, for instance, on *Days*, there was sweet and pretty Hope Brady telling dim and buff John Black (who hasn't been the same since the evil Stefano DeMira took his brain out and washed it) that she must know about her past.

"I must know, John! I must know about my past. Why don't you understand?"

"Be careful what you wish for," said John Black, raising a soap-opera brow and looking mysterious. "You just might get it."

I realized that this was the exact same conversation the two of them had one year earlier. In soap land, wedding ceremonies last four to six weeks and a prom night can go for six months so this shouldn't have come as a surprise. Paradoxically, a kid who is in kindergarten one month can mutate into a surly teenager with a pregnant girlfriend in the next.

(Hope Brady to surly teen dad: "Soooo, how long have you known this girl and are you sure you really know anything about . . . *her past?*")

In desperation, soaps have started adding a lot of ooga-booga ghost storylines with voodoo, witchcraft, and, in the case of one, a Chucky-style creepy doll that comes to life. They've given Erica Kane a lesbian daughter to lure the gay audience, and you can be sure that, sooner or later, Erica will have her daughter's brain taken out and washed so she can live a decent, normal life with seven husbands just like her mama.

There is talk that *Days* will soon be courting Hispanic viewers by including more Latino storylines. This time next year, I just know I'll kick back in front of the big TV and hear Hope Brady whining about her "el past-o" and John Black will be advising her that it was *"muy mal es verdad."*

Which, as I recall from high school Spanish, means you have to have correct change for the dryers. Or something like that.

5

SICK OF SEEING MEN
at Those "Couples" Baby Showers?

Tell 'Em About the Time You Lost Your Mucus Plug in the Winn-Dixie

A pregnant friend told me her husband has written a "birth plan" to present to the obstetrician at her next checkup.

Men love devising these birth plans because it gives them something to do in the waiting room besides pretending to read the magazine articles their wives keep shoving at them. ("Rupert, read this about inverted nipple syndrome; it's fascinating!") Birth plans also distract men from dwelling on the age-old question of why some women seem to recruit armies of small, whiny children to bring with them to every appointment.

My pregnant friend, Amy, asked me about my birth plan, and I said it had been real simple.

"Really?" she said. "Harold has several pages of plans with supporting documentation and footnotes. He's amazing. Did you manage to keep yours under two pages?"

"Well, uh, we didn't really write that much down," I said.

Did I have the heart to tell Amy the truth? That my "birth plan" consisted of one line hastily scrawled on the back of a maternity pantyhose carton? That it read "Drugs. Lots of 'em and keep 'em coming"?

She thought I was kidding and began to chuckle. And then she said that hormones-are-eating-my-brain thing that newly pregnant women say: "Oh, I don't want any drugs. I just want to have as natural an experience as possible. I don't want to miss a single second!"

Sure you do. Listen to me. If I could have, I would have been sitting on the third-base line at Dodger Stadium, roughly three thousand miles from that hospital, eating a sausage dog and swilling Bud Light during my kid's birth.

You don't want to miss a second? True. You want to miss hours. I'll let you in on a little secret, hons. The whole delivery thing is vastly overrated. Sure, you think you're going to lie up there with Mozart softly playing from the portable CD player hubby so thoughtfully packed. He's going to be rubbing your back with tennis balls rolled up in a sock while you speak in loving tones about the wonderment that is taking place in your body, your lives.

He's going to gently spoon ice chips into your alarmingly dry and crusty mouth while murmuring that you are, without a doubt, the bravest, most wonderful woman in the world.

As the time draws near, you experience some discomfort, surely, perhaps even some pain, but this is more than countered by the presence of your dear partner telling you to "Breathe, darling, just like in class."

A doctor will enter the room, and softly say, "It's time." Then, after a few soap-opera birth-scene squeals, for which you apologize profusely, presto-whammo, you've got a baby.

Birth plans are silly because they give the illusion that you have any control at all over a situation that is completely beyond your control.

I didn't say this to Amy, who has watched way too many episodes of *A Baby Story* on The Learning Channel and is convinced she wants a water birth. At home. With a midwife.

Amy insisted on wearing regular clothes throughout her pregnancy just because "all the pregnant celebrities do it."

Amy wasn't alone. Although I was happy to see the demise of the "Baby" shirts with the arrow pointing crotchward (yecch!) and the dancing bear casual/Bo Peep–collared business wear that used to define maternity fashion (as though just because we were pregnant our

IQs had inexplicably plunged 75 points), tight clothes on pregnant women look, well, tacky.

I saw Jane Leeves (*Frasier*'s Daphne Moon) at the Emmys stuffed in a painted-on sleeveless sheath that made her look like the cover girl for *White Trash Weekly*. All she needed was some Vi-enna sausages and Saltines and a *True Story* magazine.

Amy said she was proud for the world to watch her blooming body. I told her that while she thought she looked chic and fabulous, she really looked just like the tired-ass boa constrictor at the Tote-Em-In Zoo right after he had his once-a-month bunny rabbit lunch.

I finally gave up. Amy was way granola. I knew she would plant the afterbirth under a tree in her backyard and nurse her kid until it was using words like "pontificate."

She was one of the first of my friends to insist on a couples baby shower. I've been to a half dozen of these now, and the men always wear that frozen look of horror that is usually reserved for when they discover that ESPN's showing the world figure skating championships.

Men have no place at baby showers. They can never figure out how to retrieve a mini-pizza from beneath the puffy fold-out stork centerpiece and it'll break your heart to watch 'em try.

Recently, I took the dad-to-be aside and gave him some tips: "Here's the drill. You open the gift, hold it up, and squeal something like, 'It's beautiful. Oh, thank you so much. It's exactly what we wanted!'"

I even told him how you have to pass it to the person beside you so it can make the long, strange trip around the room and everyone can repeat the exact same comments. ("Why, yes! This *is* the most precious and darling breast pump I've ever seen!")

This dad-to-be finished his beer, burped, and said, "Huh? Yeah, okay. Got it."

My duty done, I returned to my rented chair and watched him help his wife open an adorable bib. He held it aloft—so far, so good—and said, "Wow. Where the hell did you get this thing?"

This is why no man should be at any party that ends in the "shower" word.

It's not their fault. We've had practice. At bridal showers, we women can gush worthy of an Oscar over a crocheted toilet paper cozy.

The men who go to these showers always abandon their buddy at the first announcement that it's present time. Utter the phrase "mucus plug" or debate the merits of Baby Bjorn over Snugli and they leave him like a wounded animal, fleeing to the room with the big TV or the deck, where they can bond over a few "foamers."

Amy's Harold had done better than most at their shower, probably because, as she frequently pointed out, "He is very much in touch with his feminine side," causing his buddies to snicker and make tent tits by pulling on their Polo knits.

As her time drew near, I felt I had to tell Amy the truth about unrealistic birth plans.

My own, highly realistic birth plan worked splendidly. The unwritten part was that I had purposely fattened my baby up like a Christmas turkey so I'd have to have a C-section (so much more civilized than all that screaming and carrying on).

The plan worked to perfection. On the appointed day, I waddled to the hospital and settled into my pillows, a fabulous epidural coursing through my spine, and (natch) *Days of Our Lives* on the overhead TV. It was positively magical.

I knew that my baby was going to be big. This much had been assured by twice-daily trips to Hardee's for chocolate twist-T cones and double cheeseburgers. What I didn't expect was that everybody in the hospital, including, I suspect, some of the janitorial staff and grounds crew, would step into the room, put on a rubber glove, root around in my naughty bits, and announce, "Whew! That's a big baby!"

I just shooed them all away because Stefano was right in the midst of unveiling an evil plan to clone John Black's baby and plant a love-inducing microchip in the brain of Salem's most esteemed Dr. Marlena Evans to win her back.

After a while, I was flapping my knees open for the frikkin' florist. I didn't care. Just let me watch my soaps. "Right," I'd mumble. "Big baby. Got it." (Delivery guy: "Whoa, lady, put that away. It's just a trailing philodendron.")

I don't know why everyone seemed so surprised at the size of my baby. That's why they call it a birth plan, right?

And, baby, everything was going according to plan. As planned, the Bulls clinched their third championship just after midnight and the doc turned to me and my hubby. "Ready?"

"Well, Jordan's gonna say some stuff in the post-game I'd like to hear," said my husband.

To tell the truth, we all wanted to hear what Mike had to say. I mean, it *was* a three-peat.

A half hour later, we were in the operating room and the doc was asking my hubby if he'd like to "come on down" like he was on *The Price Is Right* or something. Hubby blanched, then looked at me to be the heavy. Which was easy since I was in the final moments of weighing the rough equivalent of a PT Cruiser.

Come on down? The drugs were so good almost nothing could bother me. Except for the thought that my husband would see my intestines sitting around like a wriggling plate of pasta while the doc dived in for baby.

So, no. Hubby sat beside my head, where he belonged

and where we could turn to one another in utter disbelief when we first heard a weird and wonderful *"Waaaaahhhh"* and a nurse was handing us a nearly ten-pound bundle of baby girl type person. Name of Sophie.

For the next three days, I thought I was in heaven. Every meal came with a strawberry milkshake, for reasons I never understood. I had the horrible feeling that I might have been getting the wrong tray, the one that was supposed to go up to the Calista Flockhart ward.

After we got home (there was a one-day delay owing to the hospital's odd obsession with my inability to "pass gas," which hubby uncharitably joked had "never been much of a problem before," yuk, yuk, yuk) we settled into that whole baby-makes-three thing.

We quickly discovered that everyone had the same question for us: "Is she a good baby?"

This question, repeated for the entire first year of Soph's life, never failed to puzzle me. A good baby? Hell, how would I know? After a while, I just settled on the smart-ass default: "Oh, she's awful! We're thinking of sending her back before the warranty expires. *Honey!* Check that expiration again so we don't miss the deadline."

A good baby? What does that mean?

The other dumber-than-a-box-of-rocks question was "Are you getting much sleep?"

Sure, I am. I've always snored with my eyes wide open in the post office and worn my shorts inside out; why do you ask?

In the end, we made it through that first year with the help of *Nick at Nite* nurse-a-thons. The plus side of breast-feeding was that it reunited me with my old crush, Chachi, still young and handsome in those 2:00 A.M. reruns.

Because my pregnancy coincided with that of beloved frontier doctor Jane Seymour's, I felt we had a special bond when she, and her twin boys, became Gerber spokesmodels.

There were the robust twins dutifully eating their mushy food from a jar and so was Sophie. We parted company, though, when I realized that Jane Seymour's twins were still peddling Gerber graduates and Soph was already into T-bones. While Jane kept yammering about the importance of not rushing into, well, people food, Soph and I were pointing at the twins and hooting. What three-year-old eats jars of cold carrot cubes?

It was as hard to swallow as those god-awful "meat fingers" the twins were supposed to be thriving on. Mercifully, Jane's Gerber contract must've expired because the twins disappeared around age four, presumably mad as hell that they'd missed all those Happy Meals.

Once you're in the toddler years, there's a new stupid question: "Is it potty-trained yet?" I say "it" because there's no clinical evidence that a two-year-old is human, but rather has been temporarily possessed by demons that respond only to the siren song of the God of All Creation: Chuck E. Cheese.

The playground moms began to compare notes on potty-training progress but I felt this was silly. I thought a child should progress at her own pace, not some so-called pediatrician's.

In other words, I didn't have a clue.

I rented potty-training videos and checked out library books including the classic, *Everyone Poops,* and others by Dr. William Sears and Dr. T. Berry Brazelton, who disagreed on everything.

Dr. Sears thinks parents should get in there and get those kids pooping in a pot. Dr. Brazelton, the soft-spoken flower child of parenting, thinks that if your kid wants to wear diapers to his prom, no biggie. This man is so unflappable you could draw on his office walls with a set of Sharpies and he'd just smile, and say, "Aren't kids creative?" Makes me want to slap him upside his head.

Some of my mom-friends gave reward stickers for each time their kid went potty but I don't think a kid should be taught that the simple act of peeing deserves a prize. What's next? A new bike for agreeing to breathe all day?

I told Amy all this and she looked a bit pale.

Her birth plan fluttered to the floor and she didn't even notice.

"Remember," I said in my most comforting and motherly Sharon Osbourne tone, "that which does not kill us merely maims us."

Or something like that.

Part 4:
THE SOUTHERN
Woman

The Truth? We're Just Like You, Only Prettier

1

SCIENTISTS DISCOVER
Fat Virus!

**How I Went from Diet, Exercise, and Giving a Shit to
Gnawing 99¢ Turkey Legs at the Stop-n-Go**

I *can't* put it off any longer, this search for the Perfect Swimsuit. Vacation is looming and there's just
no way I'm going to wear gym shorts in the pool again
this year. Children can be so cruel.

So, here's the dilemma: Do I want the basic maillot,
the "tankini" (a bikini for tanks), a high-neck, or low-
neck? An ombre bubble or a batik with side panel slen-
derizers? A ribbed faille two-piece or a zipper tank in
color block?

Experts say that the key to successful swimsuit shopping—aside from laying off the Coronas during the winter months—is to determine your correct body shape.

Are you a "triangle," "circle," "rectangle," or "inverted
triangle," for instance? They say you are what you eat,
so I believe I'm more of a "lasagne."

Once you've established that, you can immediately proceed to the swimsuit department of your favorite store, where you will discover that they only sell suits for "straight lines" on account of most swimsuit manufacturers are designing strictly for Courteney Cox Arquette after a busy morning of bingeing and purging.

And while we're on the subject, why don't any of the big stars have a butt anymore? Have they been surgically removed? Meg Ryan used to have a butt; now she just sits on a couple of sticks. Same with Jennifer Aniston. Did they just wake up one morning and go, "Holy shit! Where's my butt?" Call the butt police and put out an APB (all pointy-butted).

This year they've tossed those of us shaped more like Camryn Manheim a bone in the form of the ultra-trendy "pareo," a color-coordinated scarf thingy that you wear over your swimsuit to disguise figure flaws and dress up a bit for poolside parties.

The pareo looks terrific until you decide to go in the water. That's when you sheepishly peel it off, drape it over your chaise, and hear the audible gasps from your friends. ("Pssst! Fat Woman Walking!")

Once you've selected a few swimsuit possibilities, you can go to the dressing room where you will, no doubt, find that the only available cubicle is right beside two giggling fifteen-year-old Brit-nees who weigh approximately ninety-seven pounds apiece. Sooner or later, they will take off their little Barbie clothes and squeal things like: *"Ohmigod!* Can you believe these thunder thighs?" to each other. I'd like to kill 'em in their sleep.

All this has the effect of keeping you from ever leaving the dressing room to make that long walk of shame toward the larger, actually useful three-way mirror down the hall.

Swimsuit shopping this year has been particularly crappy because, well, I've gained a few el-bees. I was getting pretty pissed about it all until I read about a study reported in the *International Journal of Obesity* (circulation 55,000, but it seems like more) that found a "fat virus."

Turns out, the Adenovirus 36, a fairly common human virus, was injected into lab rats "just for kicks" and, almost immediately, the rats' body fat actually doubled.

I'm imagining the rats were plenty cheesed about this, forced to cancel summer plans to loll about in little rat-kinis while looking happily bored at some hotel's lazy river.

I know I've got the fat virus and I can even tell you when I got it. I distinctly remember standing in front of the Ben & Jerry's section at the grocery store last March when a very large man sneezed on me. It was one of those big, fat-guy sneezes where he goes "Yeaaah boy!" when he's done.

And speaking of overweight men, have y'all noticed

how more men are whining about weight loss?

My husband, who is not overweight but thinks he is, recently spent most of our couples' night out discussing the fat gram contents of various breakfast cereals with his buddy.

Buddy's wife and I sat there and talked about the Panthers' chances this season. No, what I meant to say was we sat there in amazement. Is this what we have sounded like all these years and, if so, why didn't y'all tell us to shut up?

Men have discovered dieting and, trust me, it's not a good thing. Lately, my husband has taken to asking me if "these pants make my ass look too big." Coming from a man who has never worn a single item of clothing that wasn't bought for him by his mother, sisters, or me, this is scarier than spray-on hair.

When his college chum called my hubby from his new job in Australia the other night, there was a cursory discussion of college football followed by a long and obsessive counseling session about muscle-to-fat ratios, the perfect workout, and, yes, the fat content of salad dressings, which, my husband pointed out from a world away, could torpedo a perfectly nutritious salad.

Pod person, release my husband. He has morphed into a fifteen-year-old girl in an afterschool special, the one where you know her bulimic best friend's going to croak and she'll survive, barely, only to be beat up by her boyfriend over on Lifetime—Television for Women someday.

Men, if they're determined to keep up this diet talk, have a lot of catching up to do. When I hear a bunch of 'em sitting in a sports bar discussing the miracle cabbage soup diet, then I'll accept that, yes, men are the new women.

(The only miracle in that diet, by the way, is that your intestines don't technically explode; they just toy with the notion.)

We are thiiiiss close to hearing men elbow each other, and hiss, "Ever since Bob and Susie got married, he has just *let himself go!*"

It all makes me rather nostalgic for the men who used to strut the beach, nekkid Buddha belly spilling over their trunks, and not a care in the world.

"Uh!" I can imagine hubby saying. "Can you believe he walked out of the house wearing *that?*"

The fat virus theory should appeal to men dieters, too. Face it: It's far more desirable to think your weight gain is caused by a virus than a distressing tendency to order the Tex-Mex Tower o' Appetizers at Friday's and eat it all by yourself. ("Hmm? The rest of my party? Oh, they should be here any minute." Gnaw, crunch, burp.)

The way I see it, this fat virus gives me carte blanche (French for "white car") to eat anything and everything. Even a white car.

No more embarrassment about paying for a gym membership and never showing up. Why bother? People, I am *ill*. No more need for creative excuses for not exercising (bad armpit hair day, allergy to hair "scrunchies" favored by perky aerobics instructors, etc.).

As I pondered this in my new pareo, I resolved to call my friend Pam, who is obsessed with fad diets, and let her in on the great news. Lately she's been drinking a powdered batwing extract she mixes with diet Coke. She hasn't lost an ounce but her night vision is terrific.

The fat virus study found that up to 30 percent of overweight people are suffering from the virus. Oh, Lordy, give us a telethon! We can all waddle to the center court at the mall, eat butter-drenched pretzels, and beg for bucks.

Researchers are saying now that they need more study before they can decide whether it will be possible to develop a vaccine against the fat virus.

I hope they don't. I got a lot of skinny, great-looking friends I plan to sneeze on.

Once the vaccine kicks in, it will end the careers of some famous former fatties. Remember Monica Lewinsky as spokesman for Jenny Craig? ("I used to seduce world leaders in inappropriate places but ever since I lost thirty-one pounds with Jenny Craig, I date nice, normal boys my own age, drink sugar-free hot cocoa, and watch old movies for fun!")

Face it, the retooled, svelte Monica is so damned

wholesome she could land a spot on *The Waltons* if it was still on TV. (Possible *TV Guide* synopsis: "A reformed D.C. strumpet visits Walton's Mountain, causing Ma and Pa to fret that John Boy will become John Man.")

And let's not forget Fergie. One minute the Duchess of York was splashed across the tabloids in grainy photos showing her cavorting topless with some creepy Austin Powers–looking rich dude and, next thing you know, she's discovered Weight Watchers and busies herself visiting war orphans and writing sweet children's books about talking helicopters.

The message seems clear: lose twenty pounds and say good-bye forever to ho-dom!

Don't get me wrong. Bravo for anybody trying to rebuild their ruined little life, but must they do it so publicly, as though the rest of us need to remake ourselves in their image? Listen. We got fat-making meat loaf for our families, not getting our toes sucked in exotic ports o' call, or giving hummers in high places, am I right?

As if the fat virus wasn't enough great news, Pam told me (while hanging upside down in her living room) that she just learned about a study that proves that people can increase muscle power by simply "visualizing themselves doing exercise."

After she told me this, I practically burned rubber driving to the "Why" to cancel my membership. When they pointed out that I'd have to pay a couple of hundred bucks if I ever rejoined, I just laughed at them, pressed my fingertips to my temples, and visualized about seven and a half pounds off my jigglypuff thighs.

Adios batwing arms and a lower stomach that hasn't recovered since pregnancy. What is *with* that, anyway? You do those stupid crunches all morning and your lower stomach just laughs at you and slides on down the hall toward the showers. Gravity has hit your stomach so bad since pregnancy that small children ask if they can sit on a burlap sack and slide down to your feet.

But with the new visualization technique, swimsuit shopping and exercise will be fun again. Farewell elliptical trainer, kickboxing class, and "fitness ball." I'm going to have a very large and very foamy full-fat double belly-busting latte while I close my eyes and visualize an entire Pilates class.

Whoa. Imaginary sweat is falling from my brow already. This is fabulous!

Pam called me later to tell me that she'd read a followup in which the researcher insisted that the visualization technique wasn't "just an excuse for every fitness-loathing barnacle seeking to justify a movement-free lifestyle."

Well, ouch, dude.

You opened the Pandora's box of possibilities, my friend, and I'm buying. Do you imagine that the inventor of the toothbrush ever wanted us to go back to scraping our gums with tree bark?

Enough said. It's nearly time for my imaginary Tae Bo class. I really must lie down.

2

I DRUM 'EM ON MY DESK
and They Click Like a Poodle on Pergo

The Dirty Little Secret of Manicure Addiction and Other American Beauty Rituals

We women are always looking for the one product or process that will transform us into the beautiful creatures we are 'sposed to be. And that, hons, is how I got addicted to manicures.

It started innocently enough as a special-occasion set of acrylic nails for my first book signing. Knowing I would be on TV later that day, I was nervous as a hen on a hot griddle, desperate for a confidence booster.

The truth was, I wasn't used to being out in the working world. Marketing? Promotions? Book signings and talking to grown-ups? I'd given up my job at the newspaper where I'd worked for twelve years to stay home with my kid. I was used to hanging around the house talking to toddlers. Would I be able to bluff my way through acting like a grown-up again after so many years of watching, hell, *enjoying* the Tellytubbies?

Then it hit me: a set of awesomely long, cherry red nails would be just the ticket. I could fan the fakes over the cover of my book while purring about its contents. No one would notice any stammering or stumbling, they'd just say to themselves, *Grandma, what big nails you have!*

I showed up at the nail salon a few minutes early, surprised to see four other women sitting on floral slipper chairs and discussing their weekly manicures. Like any good redneck, I always thought you only got fake nails if you were getting married that afternoon.

A couple of hours later, I left wearing my new, magnificent talons, the kind where you drum them on purpose just to hear their lovely click-click, like a poodle on Pergo.

The nails did their job. I sailed through the TV interview waving my hands wildly as if conducting an imaginary symphony and slapping my cheeks a lot, *Home Alone* style. This seemed to confuse the host but who cared? The more confused he looked, the more I flapped and fanned.

The next few weeks, I realized I might have a problem. See, I'd never intended to keep going back to the nail salon but these beauties were as addictive as crack. Every time I sat in my slipper chair and presented my nails to Allison, I would try to form the words: "Just dissolve these and put some clear on my real nails" but instead, it came out as "Don't you think my pinkies could use some length?"

They say that Barbra Streisand is so nail-obsessed that she gets manicures twice a day. Hey, if you want to see somebody with a problem, look no further than Babs.

I mean it's not as if I can't quit anytime I want to. It's not like it's hurting anybody else, right? The more I think about it, it's not like I really have a problem. Maybe you all are the ones with the problem. Man.

It could be much worse.

Have you heard about people who are so beauty obsessed they go to Botox parties in their friends' homes?

Pampered Chef? See ya, wouldn't wanna be ya. Tupperware? You're just so Flock of Seagulls. This is the new millennium! Trot over to your friend's house for some Botox in the butt-ocks, or wherever you think could use a little wrinkle removal.

Botox parties are all the rage since the FDA (motto: "AIDS, hell! Isn't that a frowny-face line on your forehead?") gave its official okie-dokie to the cosmetic use of the toxin. Nowadays, plastic surgeons show up at these home parties toting boxes of Botox in their little black bags. It's not exactly the prairie house call for smallpox, is it? Then again, who knew it was this easy to get a doctor to make a house call? I'll just lure him over for an eyebrow lift and then hit him up for something for this wet, hacking cough.

This is starting to make my manicure addiction seem kind of tame, isn't it? Lucky for me, Botox parties are still more of a big-city thing, just huge in New York and L.A., where guests sip Champagne and eat caviar while they wait for injections that cost several hundred bucks. It's probably cheaper down South.

How hard can it be to make botulin toxin anyway? Isn't that the same stuff we were always warned would kill us if we ate a chicken salad sandwich that had set out in the sun too long? (As a child, this was drilled into me by elderly aunts who convinced me that a single bite of poorly preserved potato salad at a picnic would cause "death *and* permanent injury.") So here's my question: Can I duplicate the Botox injections by simply falling asleep on the beach with some deviled eggs on my forehead?

The downside to Botox is that it works by paralyzing the muscles under your skin. So, while on the inside you may be fairly bursting with joy, your face won't show it. ("I'm so happy to see you. No. Really, I am. I've never been this happy in my entire life, can't you tell? You can't? Oh, now I'm upset. No, I am furious! You can't tell?")

As you might expect, there are naysayers in the medical community. One prominent medical ethicist said the whole notion of informed consent "doesn't have the same meaning when it's in the context of wine and cheese."

I say lighten up and have some pinot grigio and a chemical peel. To tell the truth, hons, I'm not all that interested in Botox, but I do believe this could lead to a much higher calling, say, liposuction bachelorette parties or boob jobs during the neighborhood potluck.

Hey, the docs have spoken: if you billed it, they will come.

I'd be lying if I said I hadn't considered a little facial work, particularly right before my twenty-fifth high school reunion.

Allow me to set the stage. I had the perfect little black dress, f-me heels, a fab new "har" do, as we say in the South, my nails (natch!), and, hmmmm, let's see, what else? Oh yes! Pinkeye! A raging case in both eyes. I looked like a very chic possum.

A lesser woman would have come unglued by this development which, and this is the God's truth, occurred precisely forty-five minutes before the party.

"Well," I said, swirling about my husband. "What do you think?"

"What's wrong with your eyes? They look kinda, uh, weird."

Five minutes later, I was cursing the fact that I was married to a rock star instead of an ophthalmologist. (Sorry, just practicing. That was going to be the harmless little white lie for the night.)

There's just something so undignified about a practically middle-aged woman with pinkeye. I toyed with wearing sunglasses all night but this would have just led to far-flung rumors that I had some kind of drug problem, what with the hubby's business and all. I decided to tough it out and went bravely into the night armed with useless Visine and lots of Kleenex. At first, everyone assumed I was overcome with emotion at seeing so many old (very old) friends, tears streaming down my face.

The fact that half the room thought I was having some kind of emotional breakdown wasn't lost on me. This was almost more embarrassing than the pinkeye, which, by the time the DJ cranked up *YMCA* (unavoidable), had turned into a crusty mess that had effectively *glued my eyes shut!!!*

An old boyfriend who dumped me in high school wandered over wearing a comb-over and gnawing a buffalo wing. I bolted before he could ask why I appeared to be praying during the macarena (also unavoidable) *and* the chicken dance (Valley o' Death Nursing Home, here I come!). I couldn't help but notice that our nonconformist hippiefied class of '74 was depressingly good at the electric slide, which, for reasons I don't really get, is subtitled "It's electric!" which is one of those Department of Redundancy Department things.

When I returned from the dance floor, dinner was served and I was seated beside a classmate who introduced me to her husband.

"What do you do?" I small-talked.

"I'm a race car driver," he said.

I howled at this and elbowed my hubby hard in the ribs. "Right!" I shrieked. "And this guy's really a rock star!"

There was an awkward silence (you know it really is true that when you lose one sense your other senses get much sharper) until someone hissed at me, "He really *is* a race car driver, Celia."

Ooops. Well, hell. It's not as if I could see. With my eyes mostly glued shut like this, he didn't look much different from the overdone prime rib with apple ring garnish on my plate.

I went home feeling dowdy and decidedly unbeautiful. All my life, I've been short, plump, and the kind of woman that other women don't mind talking to their husbands. "More cute than pretty" as one old boyfriend once said, meaning it nicely but making me feel like somebody's new speckled puppy.

As a little girl, and to this day, actually, I always watch the Miss America Pageant on TV because it's such a beautiful fantasy. The pageant has been on my mind a lot because, this year, my home state actually has two contestants fighting to represent North Carolina.

Sure, one of them is only hanging on by a hand-beaded metallic thread but that's just because her meanie of an ex-boyfriend tattled that he had nude pictures of her. The other Miss North Carolina, who is fortunate not to have any such scoundrel in her past, is not as pretty.

I know looks shouldn't matter because of it being the Miss America Virgin Scholarship Pageant and all, but you know as well as I that nobody really believes you'd ever see a finalist with back hair or dimply thighs. (Although there was that Miss Alaska that one time . . .)

The nudie Miss North Carolina is flat-out better looking than the sincere-suited first runner-up who is hell-bent to take the crown. The runner-up is not unattractive, but she is a pale, wan little thing you'd take home to mama and certain presidency of the Junior League. The pretty one, on the other hand, has the kind of looks that pageant judges usually term "the potential for explosive hot monkey love."

So the two Miss North Carolinas are still fighting in court instead of a nice Pay-Per-View ring match at Bally's, like God intended. Hey, it's no worse than trotting them out like prize sows in sequins.

For the record, I don't buy nudie Miss N.C.'s claim that cad boy secretly snapped topless pictures of her in a dressing room and, if you do, perhaps you'd like to invest in my new pixie dust and fairy wings dotcom opportunity.

Not long ago, I read where the eighty-one-year-old Miss America Pageant's governing body (which is, I'm guessing, 40-23-34) has decided to "punch up the drama" a bit. They're no doubt weary of trying to say things like "We're looking at the inner beauty of the contestant" without milk coming out of their noses.

Inspired by the success of TV's *Survivor*, the Miss America Pageant will now allow those who didn't make it to the Top 10 (a.k.a. the rat-faced losers) to vote for the finalist they like best. Their votes will carry just as much weight as those of the pageant's prestigious judges, typically a Vegas lounge comic, long-distance spokesman Carrot Top, and the woman who invented the hair-removal goo Nads.

This should keep the girls on best behavior. Because I've never been classically beautiful, I have to tell you that I'm excited about this. If we're insanely lucky, maybe there will even be a *Survivor*-style snake-and-rat speech by one of the embittered forty, who has fled outside the convention hall and is eating chicken straight from the bucket.

As if that's not enough, my fellow beauty junkies, the Miss America Pageant has also announced that it will forgo the interview segment in which finalists pledge to promote world peace, end hunger, and fight for dress sizes that don't lie. In its place? Five current-events questions with points deducted for incorrect answers. ("No, no, Miss Texas, the Surgeon General of the United States is not 'the guy who comes on *Oprah* every Tuesday.' ")

The talent portion of the pageant, apparently in an effort not to offend any contestant who doesn't actually have any, has been renamed Artistic Expression.

I'll never stop watching the Miss America Pageant. I'm especially happy that they've cut back on the song-and-dance routines in which some aging white guy tries to busta move (more likely a hip) while leering at the scantily clad nineteen-year-old contestants who must bat their eyes and look captivated by him. Sounds like intern-recruitment day at the Capitol, doesn't it?

And I'll never stop dreaming about being "more pretty than cute." It won't be long before the next class reunion. Tummy tuck, anyone?

3

MOTHER'S DAY
Memories

Make Mine Macaroni

My earliest memory of making a handmade Mother's Day present was when I was six years old and in the first grade. Today, the gift I made back in 1963 would strike most people as a cross between repulsive and hilarious: I, along with twenty-eight classmates, lovingly pasted photographs of ourselves onto pink construction paper, then glued the paper, faceup, to the bottom of a large glass ashtray provided by our teacher.

On Mother's Day 1963, all over Wallace, North Carolina, moms of first-graders joyously opened their personalized ashtrays and, a short while later, proudly flicked the ashes from their Kents and Bel-Airs right onto our little glass-protected faces.

There we would be for years to come, captured in

black-and-white, mostly toothless and T-shirted, smiling up at our moms through a face full of butts.

Today, of course, this would never happen. Ashtrays are as un-PC as candy cigarettes.

The next Mother's Day gift I remember making began with a heavy-duty paper plate that a responsible grownup had spray-painted silver. My task was to glue glitter-soaked elbow macaroni all the way around the plate, then, using a yellow pipe cleaner, attach a wad of plastic purple grapes from the Ben Franklin store to the center of the plate. It was a vision. And it is a testimony to my mother that this work of art hung on our living room wall until long after I had finished high school, the elbows carefully dusted once a week.

As I write this, my four-year-old daughter is at her friend's house making my Mother's Day gift.

Seeing her excitement about this top-secret project shamed me as I realized that I had spent two days quietly huffing about having to buy something for my mother and mother-in-law. Not because they don't deserve gifts, but because I had waited until the last minute and that meant a robe and slippers or maybe a purse or perfume.

Knowing that my daughter had planned, perhaps for weeks, to surprise me with what will probably involve colored feathers, small pebbles she has been picking up in the alley beside our house, and her beloved sequins, made me sad that I hadn't been just as excited.

As corny as it sounds, my proudest possession on earth is last year's Mother's Day present, a silver box from Eckerd Drugs, which my daughter secretly decorated with blue, yellow, and pink pony beads and a snowstorm of glitter. It holds every piece of jewelry I own. And it always will.

I am fairly certain neither my mother nor my mother-in-law would like a photographic ashtray, but it pains me that I ended up putting so little thought into their gifts. Grab it. Get it wrapped. Get it mailed. Mark it off the list.

Will they like their gifts? Of course. Will they be so moved that their throats close up a little when they see what's inside this box wrapped by some other woman's daughter at the store's customer service counter? Probably not.

I resolve to do better next time, to recapture some of the macaroni magic, if just for old time's sake. I am not a crafty person and marvel at the mom at my daughter's ballet class who spends our thirty-minute wait in the hallway explaining how she uses wet tea bags to age linen and make elegant picture frames.

It's unfortunate, but she is simply too nice to hate.

So the macaroni magic will not be craft induced for me. Maybe not for you either. It can be simply sitting and talking under the sycamore tree in the backyard of the home you grew up in.

One day, it will be my daughter who will be scowling

in line at the gift-wrap counter, and she will have long forgotten a sunny May afternoon when she was four and so excited about her Mother's Day project that she couldn't even sleep the night before.

That's life. I know it. And I know something more: that on those long days when we in the sandwich generation feel squeezed and spent and are tempted to grouse about being either mother or daughter, we should be fall-on-our-knees grateful to be both.

Because the truth is simple. Our time is fleeting and dear. As a good friend explained it, one day it is our mother who is buying us the Chatty Cathy that we begged for; the next, or so it seems, we find ourselves taking a baby doll as a gift to a mother in the nursing home. It has always struck me that women in nursing home beds almost always have baby dolls in their rooms. I suspect it is because they remind them of the happiest time of their lives. I know it is mine.

One day, in a hospital room somewhere, you will hold a hand that you can't even recognize anymore. It may be thin and dry and tiny, the rings way too big even with the guards you bought for her at the jewelry store.

Look closer and you'll recognize the hand that pushed you in the swing, the one that felt your burning forehead when you were sick, the one that stroked your hair the first time you had your heart broken and cried for a solid three hours.

For all of you mothers, for all of you who want to be mothers, for all of you "other mothers" who nurture children not your own, may you have a lifetime of Mother's Days filled with your own brand of macaroni magic.

I plan to.

4

"WHAT WE HAVIN' FOR DINNER TONIGHT, *Sugar Booger?*"

And Other Wildly Important Uses for the Cell Phone

I haven't weighed in on the cell phone debate because I own one and, frankly, whining about others who use them seems hypocritical even by humor-columnist standards, which are pretty lax, by the way.

But all that has changed. My phone will soon be returned to the apostate of hell, er, sales clerk who sold it to me, along with the shredded remnants of the (ha-ha) contract that guaranteed the roaming rates wouldn't go up for a year. Once, I tried to complain about my bill, which had mysteriously doubled, and was told to wait in a special line. *The line that never moves.* How long was my wait? Let's just say that Vice President Dick "I'm with Stupid" Cheney could've had a couple of dozen heart attacks in less time than it took me to work my way to the head of the line.

(And, politics aside, you gotta respect a guy who can have an angioplasty or two before breakfast and be back at his desk before the big guy has dipped his pinkie toe in the Rose Garden lap pool and polished off his power muffin.)

Before I began to hate my cell phone provider, my husband asked his niece to program the phone to play, quite loudly, "Take Me Out to the Ball Game." He did this because, at age twelve, she already knows more about cell phones than anyone we know. Lucy even programmed my name to flash on the screen, apparently in case I ever forget who the hell I am.

She told me that I could play cool games on my cell phone but I told her that probably won't ever happen since it takes three separate pairs of glasses just to be able to find the redial button.

Cell phones are great for emergencies but they are maddening when used for stupid stuff.

There was a triathalon (Latin for "must can't afford a car") in our town recently and I saw one of the participants running and talking into his cell phone. What is *that*? The ocean swim segment must've been a bitch.

I was in Target the other day and couldn't escape the loud ramblings of a cell phone addict.

"*Ohmygod*, Tiffany, you should *see* these little fountains; they are sooo cool. Huh? Oh, I'm on aisle nine. Yeah. Okay, now I'm looking at these plants that kind of look like ficus trees or something. Okay, now there's this really cool pillow that I think would look good on my bedroom on account of it's fuchsia. Huh? *Fuchsia!* Hell-o, it's like hot pink?"

My mom-friends are pathetically addicted to their cell phones. Rarely do we go to the park that their purses don't start ringing. Usually, and I have never understood this, it's the husband.

Why do some married people call each other all day long? I used to work with a woman who made at least five calls a day to her hubby on her cell phone. He did the same, so all day long anyone unfortunate to be within earshot learned that the dog had some kind of worm, hook or ring or tape, I forget which; hubby was "bored" at work; their sod isn't "taking" in the backyard like it did in the front and root rot is suspected; and wifey had developed what the commercials call painful trapped gas after eating a chimichanga from the office vending machine. Which just shows you what a lunatic she was.

At the park recently, my friend slammed her cell phone shut, and announced, "My husband calls me all day and he has absolutely nothing to say."

All over the park, you could hear the chatter. "We're at the park. Huh? At the swings. Yeah, we're going to head on over to the monkey bars in a minute. Huh? Meat loaf. No. No. Guess again. No. Butterbeans!"

The weirdest sight I see is redneck guys on cell

phones. There's just something profoundly unsettling about a guy with a mullet chatting *like a girl* into his little Barbie dream phone.

The other day, I got behind a babbling Bubba who talked all the way through his quarter-pounder and Shamrock Shake order ("Thanks, darlin', keep the change") and never stopped talking while he ate, special sauce dribbling off his bouncing chin.

Here's another scary thought.

Next time you're in the grocery and hubby calls your cell phone to remind you to pick up some athlete's foot powder and a six-pack of Coronas, you could think that you're in for a fun time tonight, but what you don't realize is that you could be partially responsible for a serious breach in that old bugaboo, National Security.

Turns out that the technology that allows us to enjoy our God-given right to talk with our friends while bummed in traffic actually leaves "radar holes" that expose the stealth bomber.

Picture it. The stealth bomber is supposed to be, well, stealthy. Because of these cell-phone-caused radar holes, the bomber's up there, squealing and doubled over, trying to cover its naughties.

One minute you're calling your mama to ask if she'd mind coming over Saturday night so you can go see *Charlie's Angels 3* with your baby's daddy and the next minute Saddam sees the stealth missile headed his way and blows it into bits. Sure, it's fab that you've got a sitter lined up, but at what cost, little missy?

This is the second shocking bit of news I've heard lately about cell phones. The other? The Amish use them.

A proud people who can actually use "shun" as a verb without cracking themselves up, the Amish don't even use zippers because they think they're too high-tech. Now they're going to be just as annoying as the rest of us.

Welcome to the shallow end of the gene pool, my hat-haired friends. There is room for all of thee.

Somehow, the mental picture of an Amish farm boy riding into town in the family buggy in his button-crotch woolen knickers isn't nearly as quaint when you realize he's talking on his cell. ("Yes, Percival, we harvested fifty acres today and tomorrow Mom's going to make one hundred and eighty-seven cobblers for the tourons. What? Oh, yes, that new Xbox kicks some major—whoa, Bessie! Sorry, Percy. She just trampled another loser with one of those goofy cardboard cameras. Hell-o. Why don't these morons go digital?")

Technology has gotten completely out of hand, if you ask me. I recently read about a security device that uses high-tech computer radar to see through clothing. It can spot concealed weapons from as far as fifty feet away.

The "remote frisk" can be used in large crowds to spot

terrorists, but privacy nuts are concerned that, if it falls into the wrong hands, it could be used to spot exceedingly large balambas instead. I don't care how much they crow about screening the applicants for security jobs, you just know they're going to end up hiring the feebjock you went to junior high with who pestered you on the school bus everyday to show him your ta-ta's.

I'm not sure which of all these reports is the most troubling but I don't really care all that much. The truth is, it's foot powder and Corona night at my house and I'm feeling lucky.

5

REAL SIMPLE MAGAZINE: MEET MANWICH,
the Working Girl's Best Friend

How to Feng-Shui Your Way to Di-Vorce Court

*H*ave *you* seen *Real Simple* magazine yet? It looks
a lot like *Martha Stewart Living* with page after
luscious page of lovely foods and happy, real simple people wearing expensive clothes and smiling at how simple
their lives are.

"Tra-la-la," they seem to be saying as they clink simple,
elegant glasses together while wearing simple, elegant
monochromatic clothing.

The only problem is you can tell just by looking at
them that life is Real Simple only because there's a Ros-
ita somewhere taking care of the kids while they enjoy
"soul-nurturing ritual times."

Whatever the hell that means.

Real Simple is supposed to be a classy antidote to
magazines like Martha's that encourage us to spend our

spare three and a half minutes a day sponge-painting terra-cotta pots with yogurt in order to cultivate a "distressed" look. (Look closer, toots. That's me, not the pot, looking distressed.)

According to its editors, the magazine was created to "provide beautiful, actionable solutions for simplifying every aspect of your life."

Words like *actionable* leave me feeling unsimple and even anxiously complicated. Much the same way I felt while reading the "Pantry Dinners" section of the magazine and discovered that their idea of a simple recipe for Vegetable Chili with Polenta contained thirteen ingredients, not a danged one of them in my pantry.

What? You people never heard of Manwich?

Another issue printed a recipe for a tuna casserole that didn't even include cream of mushroom soup, proving that they've got a lot to learn about the simple life.

Real Simple is shameless in its quest to simplify everything. There's even a section called "Soul—In a Nutshell," apparently for people who are overcome by the rigorous demands of developing a soul via Oprah's three-minute "Remembering Your Spirit" segments. Shouldn't some things take a little time?

Real Simple seeks to remind the frazzled working woman and mom that "It's about quality, not quantity." Less is more, they say.

No, it's not. More is more. Their idea of a lovely table

is one white candle plunked down in the middle? I'm glad these freaks didn't plan my wedding reception, where every table had enough flowers for a casket spray.

It's quite trendy now to take decorating advice from "minimalists." Take ikebana, for instance. This is a type of flower arranging where you essentially take a big stick from your yard, wire a single flower to it, and charge fifty bucks. I don't get it.

With this simplicity movement comes the new national obsession: "nesting" at home. Whatever happened to going out on the town, spending too much money, and staying out too late?

I'm sick of all those magazine articles about the importance of pot-roast-and-mashed-potato family dinners. I can't honestly believe that macaroni and cheese is the best way to soothe our national psyche. Nope. I want to go out on Friday night and have somebody serve me something sumptuous that isn't topped with Tater Tots. This is what it means to be an American, not sitting around weaving and discussing everybody's damn day. Don't we do that enough the rest of the week?

The whole return to the nest has led to a new design trend: the "hearth room." This is what we used to call the living room, that oversized, underfurnished, and always-cold-in-the-winter room where nobody ever went unless it was Christmas or piano-lesson time.

Later the living room morphed into the "family room"

and, finally, the "great room." We have a small one so I just call it the "okay room."

The new "hearth room" is a kitchen/great room combo that actually includes a fireplace where you can tend those stewpots on Friday night instead of going out and getting sloppy on licorice margaritas like you used to do until They decided we should spend Fridays mixing cookie dough with the kids.

Now, don't get me wrong. I love cookie dough, but adults deserve some downtime, away from all that hearth and kith and kin. Or you can kith your sanity good-bye.

The hearth room is supposed to call to mind the home-spun life so revered in shows like *The Waltons*. One big room with Grandma rolling out lard biscuits while John Boy scribbled obsessively on the settee.

Designers should remember that there was a reason everybody hung out in one hearth room back then. It was the Depression, that dark time in our nation's history when nobody ever had a date. Better to remember that those who don't learn from history are doomed to spend Friday nights at home. Or something like that.

Aside from the silly hearth room, there's the huge trend of "feng shui," which is pronounced fung schway just to play with your head. In a soulful nutshell, this promotes moving your furniture and pictures and stuff around to create a harmonious environment that will "grow" your spirit.

A friend begged to give my house a fung schway make-over. She said our wealth was "just a-flyin' out of the house" because we had a deck on the back that was, unfortunately, smack in the middle of our "wealth quad-rant" and this meant there was nothing to harness the financial energy and keep it from running like a madman into the street.

She was also distressed to see that the closet on the northeast corner contained coats, a vacuum cleaner, brooms and mops, assorted skates, and a Wiffle ball set. She said this was chaotic, and I said, what's your point? It's not like I can walk around all day with this stuff strapped to my back or a shopping cart. I mean, that's okay for some members of my family but not for me.

Moving upstairs, she was horrified to see the TV in our bedroom and suggested that we replace it immedi-ately with candles and treasured books, with everything facing east.

She meant well but she was talking nutty as a three-ingredient *Real Simple* fruitcake. Trust me, hon, I told her. Without ESPN in the bedroom, there will be no harmony. So there.

I told my husband all about our free fung schway con-sultation that night and I don't think he understood. He just said that if I was thinking about fung schway to please be sure to order a couple of extra spring rolls because I always eat the baby shrimp out of his. (And where do they get those anyway? Do they make 'em smoke when they're young?)

Fung schway isn't new, of course, but the whole *Real Simple* anti-Martha movement has given it new life.

True believers love that this ancient Chinese art of decorating is based on promoting balance, harmony, light, and inner peace, as opposed to our style of decorating, which is based on moving the furniture in front of wherever you couldn't scrub the Magic Marker off the wall.

Fung schway has its place, I guess. Why else would so many people turn to respected FS expert Angi Ma Wong who writes columns about this, answering the questions of angst-filled readers who fear that their BarcaLoungers and buffets are out to get them?

In one column I read, Ms. Wong addressed the question of whether it would be okay to install mirrored closet doors in the bedroom, even though the mirrors would face the windows, a huge fung schway no-no.

Ms. Wong's answer, written in the time-honored Magic 8 Ball style, said "It is not advisable" to put mirrored doors in the bedroom "especially if they reflect any part of your body while you're in bed." (Amen to that!) She pointed out that mirrors move energy around and since the soul does its astral traveling while you're asleep it might get "startled by seeing its image in a mirror." I don't know about y'all, but I usually tell my soul to just stay put while I'm sleeping. As long as I let it watch the occasional *Law and Order* rerun first, it's usually perfectly happy to settle down for the night.

Another letter tackled fung schway for the home office. Ms. Wong says that if you use your home computer to earn money, it should be located in the southeast corner of your home. Well, this explains a lot. My computer has faced northwest for years now but I have since moved it based on Ms. Wong's recommendation and should be insanely wealthy by the time you read this so, Prize Van, ease on down da road.

Ms. Wong advised another reader that open bookcases may direct negative "sha" energy toward the occupants of your living room, causing injury or pain to the body part the edges are pointing toward. This explains all those guests who, over the years, have reached for another Tostito, then collapsed in a heap. I always assumed it was my salmon dip.

Sha energy? Shee-it.

All of this makes me pine, almost, for my *Martha* magazines. Martha is the Antichrist of simple. Or maybe she's just the Antichrist, period. I finally let my subscription lapse after she made me feel irrationally guilty for not sewing my own shower curtain.

When Martha got in trouble for insider trading a while back, I never worried that she'd suffer. Martha is a survivor and, while it would be a little odd to pen *Martha*

Stewart Living from the pen, I knew that Martha would not only find the silver lining but grab it by the corners, stuff it with free-range goose feathers, and embroider it with silk thread produced by millions of tiny silkworms she tended in her prison windowsill.

While *Real Simple* would embrace the chic minimalist beauty of the cell, Martha would find all sorts of ways to find the "good thing-ness" of her new home.

I sent Martha some magazine ideas I came up with just in case she'd actually do jail time.

In "Woodworking for Survival" Martha could share techniques for carving and painting decorative shivs for use in shower stall encounters of the unpleasant kind. (Just because it's a weapon that can remove one's spleen with a flip of the wrist doesn't mean it has to be unsightly!)

In "Prison Laundry This!" Martha would demonstrate fabric-softening techniques that transform that eighty-thread-count prison sheet into something as supple as Egyptian cotton. Sidebar: "How to Fold a Fitted Sheet," a skill she has often demonstrated on TV, empowering millions of women to try, give up, and ultimately stuff 'em back into the linen closet in a flowery wad and start drinking because "it's five o'clock some-damn-where."

In "Growing Just About Anything from Seeds!" Martha could rely on help from her new prison friend, Bertha, to secure seeds to produce lush, hardy plants that, when smoked in the rec yard, would ensure a voracious appetite for the evening meal of Noodleroni and canned fruit cup.

In "Doing What You Have to Do," Martha could share how a few moments of mindless sex with a prison guard helped her acquire lavender water for her hand-tatted pillowslips and a smallish Vulcan range.

In "Doing What You Have to Do—Part II," Martha adds a Sub-Zero refrigerator, a set of Calphalon cookware and a case of seventy-year-old balsamic vinegar.

In "Basic First Aid," Martha could demonstrate how to dress a scalp wound properly while advising readers that, when asked what a mandoline is, simply explain that it is a French kitchen tool for making perfect angular slices of vegetables and fruits, rather than ask, "What were you? Raised by wolves?"

Those Berthas can turn on you, you know. Simple as that.

6

SCREW THE WISDOM OF
Menopause

A friend confided to me recently that she wasn't sure if it was the "change," plain old PMS, or just a slow shift toward embracing her inner witch that is causing her to become progressively more irritated by everything her husband does.

I laughed when she suggested this irritation might be a sign of menopause because, as I reminded her, we are exactly the same age, which is *way* too young for that. And on an unrelated subject, why doesn't anybody in this rathole I call a house ever turn the air conditioning on? You could fry a steak on my face, for heaven's sake.

But where was I?

Oh yes. My friend said that she realized just last week that her husband chews his food "funny, from side to side, with his chin wobbling left to right like it's playing its own little table-tennis game."

When she complained to him, suddenly and explosively one morning—"Why do you have to eat like that? It is driving me insane, you thoughtless prick!"—hubby just looked puzzled. Using so-called logic, he said very calmly, "I have been chewing this way my whole life and you never said anything about it before."

"Your whole life? How the hell would I know about your whole life? Do I have to remind you one more time that *I am not your mother!*"

The next day, the bestselling self-help book, *The Wisdom of Menopause*, appeared on her nightstand, still in its Barnes & Noble bag. This, incidentally, constitutes gift wrap to most men.

The Wisdom of Menopause is very popular among women in my age bracket, which, now that I've turned forty-five, is more cruel than I realized. Consider the age breakdowns on a typical warrantee card you might fill out for your new hair dryer or toaster oven: Your Age (please check one): 18–24; 25–44; 45–100 . . .

I haven't read *The Wisdom of Menopause* because the title sounds like New Age crap. Every time I hear a fifty-something friend crow about how she's finally old enough to explore her inner self and really get to know who she is in this life, I tell her I'm sure she'd trade all that self-awareness in a nanosecond for a chance to be a fit and bra-less twenty-six doing Jell-O shots with Jude Law.

Don't get me wrong. I'm a lot wiser than I was in my twenties, but wisdom, my friends, is overrated. Now I know that I'm on the slippery slope of deteriorating eyesight and memory thanks to lunches with women friends that are dominated—I swear—by discussions of the benefits of regular colonoscopies.

I could snap Katie Couric's perky little neck for getting us all started on that. I haven't been able to watch the *Today* show ever since a tiny camera went into her celebrity colon on live TV while I was trying to eat my apple-cinnamon Waff-Fulls.

I can't have a ten-minute conversation with my women friends lately without somebody dragging their colon into it. It practically needs its own chair at the restaurant ("Will your colon be having anything or is it just along for the ride?"). Ten years ago it was the importance of having regular "mammy-o-grams" as elderly Southern women insist on calling them, making it seem as if some kindly, kerchiefed Aunt Jemima is going to be the one that squishes our dinners (that's Southern for breasts) in that X-ray gizmo.

Mammy-o-grams? Colonoscopies? What ever happened to mindless gossip and trash talking over a plate of overpriced arugula? I mean, this is still America, the last time I checked.

When I was growing up, menopause was pointedly ignored in polite company. How I pine for those days when everybody instinctively knew to tiptoe around cranky Aunt Hettie because she was going through "the change."

The first time I heard the expression, I asked in my nine-year-old innocence, "What change?" and was told what every decent grown-up should say at times like this: "You'll find out one day." Asked and answered, I returned to the task of trapping lightnin' bugs in a Duke's mayonnaise jar. No one of any age dwelled on such personal matters.

Instead, Aunt Hettie took to sitting on her front porch in nothing but her slip, anxiously fanning herself with one of those church fans that has the praying hands on the front and the name of the funeral home on the back.

It wasn't a pretty sight.

But that's the point; menopause isn't pretty. It's—from what I'm told—night sweats, diminished mooney-gooney, sleeplessness, irritability, pure hell. Sure, some women might have an easier time of it than others, leaving fantasies about plunging the Fiskars into their husband's ears all the way up to their orange handles to the truly whacked-out meno-chicks.

While I'm not technically "changing" just yet, I know it won't be long. I've slipped into a she-who-must-be-obeyed mindset for a few months now. Okay, years. Little things that have no business bothering me drive me nuts. Like how, no matter how often I ask, my husband never shuts a cabinet or closet door. This means I must systematically go through the entire house slamming doors like Joan Crawford on crank and sobbing: "How (*slam*) inconsiderate (*slam*) can one (*slam*) person (*slam*) be?"

I shouldn't wonder that he can't shut doors because he can't see things right in front of his own eyes. Why else would he ask me where his shoes are (in the closet) or the eyedrops (tee-hee, in the oven) as though my ovaries are endowed with superhuman powers allowing me to see behind closed doors and drawers?

My friend Michelle swears that the worst thing about being a man is that you'd have to be married to a woman, and while we always laugh at this because it is so deliciously eat-your-young mean, she may have a point.

We women do go through the change, but it's not just with menopause, it's when we have kids and we give up any attempt at being calm or practical, and become, overnight it seems, screaming, horror-tale-spinning banshees.

My friend Terri sings in the church choir, speaks softly and sweetly to everyone she meets, and doesn't allow her children to watch cartoons in case they're violent. Yet, when pushed by the sight of her toddler straying a little too close to the highway, she quickly mutates into a bellowing lunatic, weaving tales of terror that would make Stephen King clutch his binky and sleep with a night-light.

One afternoon, as our kids played together, this gentle mom suddenly paused in the middle of a story about a canned food drive.

"Hey!" she shouted to the kids. "If you two get any closer to that road, an eighteen-wheeler is going to hit the both of you and turn you into hamburger and it'll take a dozen paramedics using Rubbermaid *spatulas* to scrape all your guts off the highway!"

The kids moved closer to us, their faces drained of color. Turning to me, my friend said brightly, "You know we've started our food drive for the homeless if you're interested. . . ."

I couldn't really hear her because I was still in shock at the mental picture of hamburger guts and spatulas. Plus, I think I wet myself.

Another friend smugly recalled that when her older child kept darting across the street in their subdivision, apparently without looking both ways, she purchased the biggest pumpkin she could find—a twenty-six-pounder—then called her son outside and proceeded to gun her engine and run over the pumpkin with her mini-van, back and forth, back and forth, creating a mass of stringy orange goo in the middle of the road.

"There!" she called to him triumphantly. "That's your head after you've been hit by a car. Any questions?"

He plays indoors a lot now.

You could ask if this is a good idea, this notion of scaring kids into being more cautious. But then we'd know you don't have kids. Because when you have 'em, you do what you gotta do.

It doesn't matter if you're the biggest natural-fibered, hairy-underarmed granola head on the street, sooner or later, you're going to say—as I did when my daughter decided to hop on one foot on the arm of the sofa—"Hey! You fall off that couch and your brains are going to start pouring out of your ears and the cats will have to lick them up!"

She silently lowered herself from the perilous perch and announced that she was "saw-wee" and would only do such dangerous things on her "birfday" from that moment on.

So, no, we don't always wait for menopause for the profound changes to our personalities; they begin, for many of us, the very moment that the nurse's aide in the flowery top and crisp white pants locks the wheelchair and helps us, pink or blue bundle in arms, into the car and our new life.

Menopause? Bring it on. I'm a mommy and I don't scare easy.

7

BIRTHDAY GREETINGS
from the Insurance Ghouls

Just Count the Rings Around My Stomach and Mail Me a Kate Spade Purse

The thing I dislike about birthdays is that, ever since I turned forty, the life insurance ghouls send me "birthday greetings" every year.

Disguised as a cheery "Congratulations!" I only have to read as far as the third paragraph to discover that, amazingly enough, I can still qualify for life insurance ("No salesman will call!") even as I must surely be lining up for earlybird specials at 4:00 P.M. and calling all the men I know "Mr. Bob Barker."

There's something depressing about the fact that I have to remind my husband that my birthday's coming up at least two months in advance, yet someone I don't even know, sitting at a computer in Globe Life Insurance's Oklahoma City headquarters, is all too glad to send me birthday greetings, right on time.

I am told, in this "birthday card," that I can—oh, joy!—take out life insurance on myself. In their words: "Give yourself and your family a birthday present that won't break, go out of style, or wear out."

Well, who the hell cares about them? Isn't this *my* birthday? Isn't this a time when we should be thinking about *me*? I'm thinking good books, nice-smelling lotions, a few CDs, maybe a Kate Spade purse. If my husband gives me burial insurance for my birthday, I can assure you he'll need it a hell of a lot sooner than I will.

The Globe Life "birthday message" continues: "When you die, this protection will go a long way toward meeting the debts you leave behind."

When you die?!?

Excuse me, Mr. Mark McAndrew, president of Globe Life, but when your wife has a birthday, I'll bet you're loads of fun. Here's poor Mrs. McAndrew, all dressed up and just praying you'll take her out to dinner at one of those Japanese restaurants where the table chef only knows enough English to call everybody "Joe" (even the women) but can catch a tossed lemon on the tines of a fork held behind his back. And here's you, cheerfully telling her, "Dear, when you die . . ."

This most recent birthday message, in which I'm led to believe that Globe Life's entire staff has been laying awake at night worried slam to death about my poor bereaved survivors, informs me that a "Birthday Life" policy can pay for my entire funeral.

Now, there's a picker-upper! It's almost as wonderful as discovering ear hair.

Birthdays should be indulgent and splendid. A day where you vow to not answer a single question beginning with "Honey, where's my . . . ?" Sure, my husband will go to work wearing his swim trunks for underwear, but that's not my problem.

Birthdays are the time to shop in the Juniors department because you can't stand being a Signature Woman, Today's Woman, or Big Fat Hag Woman. (My definition of total frustration? Cher in Talbot's. Think about it.)

It's a day to use bath products without the first name "Mister" or a cap shaped like Tigger.

Insurance companies in general are irritating entities, which leads me to share with you a letter I wrote, which you might want to adapt for your own use.

Dear Mr. or Ms. Insurance Person:

I realize that you are, by the very nature of your job, a Very Busy Individual and you probably just want to grab some lunch and watch All My Restless Children *in the break room before spending the afternoon rejecting more claims, so I'll keep this brief.*

Mr. or Ms. Insurance Person, I would just like to say that, unlike most of the disenchanted American public, I hold you and your ilk in the highest regard. How frustrating it must be to sit, day after thankless day, reading claims detailing so-called "illnesses" and "accidents" and having to deny payment for the selfsame reason a dog licks his naughties—because you can.

Sure, eventually you will probably pay some, if not all, of the claim, but what's the fun in doing so in a timely manner? You know for a fact that, more often than not, we'll just give up and pay the bill out of sheer exhaustion. Like trying to find a gas pump that doesn't have the thingy broken off or a fat-free salad dressing that doesn't taste like joint compound, some things will just never be within human grasp.

Yes, you are right when you say, "Duh, that treatment stuff costs money, buddy-ro," but, and I mean this in the most respectful way possible, isn't that why we're paying premiums? Isn't that why they call it insurance?

I apologize. I'm on a rant here, but ever since you decided that I no longer needed my anti-anxiety medication, things have been a bit tense. Even you must admit that it's a tad peculiar that the only medications on your "approved" list any-

more are corn pads and snakebite kits.

Truly, not many folks appreciate your dili-
gence. While the untrained observer might think
you're being cruel to demand "prior approval"
before you pay for an emergency-room visit, I believe that if you've got time to go get yourself a
burst appendix, you've certainly got time to call
your company's handy toll-free number and ask,
between spasms of debilitating pain, if it would
be okay to have some life-saving surgery.

Take your time; we'll wait.

What's that? If we want to hear the options
menu again, we must press 2? No, we don't want
to hear the menu again. We just want to talk to
that nice, be-sweatered man in your commercials
who is playing in piles of leaves with his kids
and saying how much he values his clients. Put
him on the line.

Uh-oh. You say we're not covered because there
was a "preexisting condition" that led to the appendix problem, that weren't we warned back in
Miss Mallard's third-grade that we should not eat
peanut shells because one day they would all col-
lect in our appendix and cause it to burst?

And didn't we continue to eat peanuts, and
therefore, minute bits of shell, at ballparks and
moviehouses across the land, thumbing our col-

lective noses at our appendix, which was, at that very second, a ticking time bomb swelling to the size of an enraged calzone? You're right. It's all our fault. Forget we mentioned it. And have a nice day.

And let's not forget the homeowners' insurance companies who have lots of nifty slogans ("Nationwide Is On Your Side," "You're in Good Hands with Allstate," "Your Policy Doesn't Cover Jack, Jill.").

That last is on my mind because an eighty-year-old sewer pipe exploded in our basement smack in the middle of our neighborhood Candlelight Christmas tour and we were told by all insurance companies concerned that two feet of swirling raw sewage isn't covered because it's considered an Act of the Devil.

Allow me to set the scene: hundreds of holiday revelers dressed in cute Christmas sweaters and gleefully consulting their homes-tour guidebooks turned onto our street and, well, lost their appetites.

Hons, this was no aroma of baking gingersnaps or bayberry candles. This was, well, shit. And it was coming from our house. In our basement.

Yes, Virginia, there might be funnier things than having the fire department arrive in full, buff splendor (the only bright spot) to make sure it was safe to light the hundreds of luminaria lining our street, but I'd be hard-pressed to think of any.

As it turned out, a city sewer pipe that had been buried twenty-five feet below the alley beside our house had ruptured and the, er, contents had found their way into our basement.

After weeks of wrangling with our insurance company and the city's, we were told that we'd have to eat the $6,000 in expenses. The city's insurance company actually told us that it was denying our claim because we failed to notify them that there was a leak in the pipe.

Considering it took twelve men five hours to dig under the alley and find the pipe, this was pretty damned funny to us. ("Honey, did you check for possible faults in the old sewer pipe buried deep beneath the alley beside our house? You didn't? Oh, that's right, it's my night to check it.")

On the other hand, it wasn't an altogether bad experience. We got to live in a motel for six weeks, a cheap one, where my favorite eavesdropped conversation was when one maid was telling another a long tale about being in a fight and ended it with "And that was the *second* time I got stabbed with a cheese knife."

Now, I'm wondering here, what are the odds? Most of us live our entire mundane little lives without getting stabbed by a cheese knife even once.

The other bright spot was learning about plumbers. Oh, insurance companies, if you had done your job in a timely, efficient, and humane manner, we might have missed out on meeting so many plumbers.

We called five of them.

"Whew!" they all said. "What's that smell?"

You'd think they'd recognize it by now. Anyway, we quickly learned that when you live in an old house, you discover that there are two types of plumbers. The first is fresh-faced, wears many cell phones and pagers, and drives a new truck with no pipes on it. These plumbers will run screaming back to their laptops and time-shares when they see octogenarian plumbing.

They only do "new construction." They take early lunch breaks for things like foccacia sandwiches and chai. They are weenies.

The second kind of plumber arrives with three days' stubble, scary-looking stains on his shirt, dirty boots, and a rusty truck loaded down with all manner of hoses and pipes. He never answers the cell phone buzzing away in his truck. It's a Christmas present from his wife, who dutifully charges it every night in hopes that one day he might actually answer it. These plumbers take no lunch at all most days because they're mucking around in the basement of a house on the coast, elegantly cussing the long-dead idiot who decided *that* was a good idea.

A friend summed it up thusly: "When it comes to

plumbers, no butt crack, no good." To that wisdom, I'd just add, "When it comes to insurance companies, they're just all butt cracks."

These are the bottom-feeders, friends, the ones who are right down there with telemarketers who sucker gullible idiots into buying property in exchange for some cruddy three-night stay in a roach motel and a busted 35-mm camera that cost them about 23¢.

Makes me want to curl my fingers around a cheese knife and just let nature take its course. . . .

Part 5:

THE GRAVY ON THE

Grits

Boobalicious Speaks Out!

1

STAMP OUT
Gossip?

My Best Friend's Mama's Sister's Hairdresser's Cousin
Won't Like This a Bit

A *bunch* of Hollywood celebrities have joined a new movement to—and it's almost too horrible to put the words into print—*stamp out gossip.*

In these times of hyperpatriotism, this is bad news indeed. Gossip, like grilling in silly aprons and whining about our cable bill, is as American as it gets. Without it, we'd all wander around talking about the weather or, worse, one another's root canals or inflamed bunions.

Bor-ing.

I'll tell you something else. Celebrities, most of whom are a bunch of Vicodin-addicted wife swappers, have no business getting involved in causes. They just look silly. Just because one has great pipes (Babs Streisand) doesn't qualify one to do much of anything except lounge about the pool between bookings and ponder the wisdom of marrying a man who brags in public about shopping at Big Lots (Jim "Tan in a Bottle" Brolin).

It's very trendy to slam gossip these days, but let me be the first Brave American to stand up at the metaphorical water cooler, and say, "Hooey!"

Gossip is the very foundation upon which this great country was built. Who knows where we'd be if a certain G.W. hadn't slept around in every little B&B on the eastern seaboard, wooden teeth happily soaking in a glass beside the bed?

Sure, gossip can be malicious and has been known to destroy lives and careers but, hey, nothing's perfect. You don't see me boycotting McDonald's just because of the McRib, do you?

The Words Can Heal movement has been embraced by a bunch of politicians. I feel better already. And I'm certain Gary Condit—y'all remember the adulterous poofy-haired louse—must be breathing a huge sigh of relief.

Of course, there's really no reason for us gossipmongers to fret. I remember a few weeks back when Oprah (who, I heard, may really be a man) had a show in which she explored the evils of gossip and pledged her own self to just stop it.

Fast forward to the next day's episode when she's asking Nicole Kidman if it's true that Tom Cruise has webbed feet.

So what happened to the Cruise-Kidmans anyway? They say they never see each other because both have such busy film careers. One wonders when they managed to see their two freshly adopted children, but then one doesn't want to sound judgmental. Oh, sure one does.

Nicole had bragged, right before the breakup, that they were "well past the seven-year itch" and that their marriage was super-solid in its eleventh year. Of course, it was solidified in the way most of ours are: by trotting around our naughty bits for all the world to see in a perfectly ghastly Stanley Kubrick movie.

The Cruise-Kidmans sued the tabloids for saying they needed a sex therapist to coach them on those steamy scenes in *Eyes Wide Shut* and won the suit. But remember what my aunt Sudavee always said: "A bit dog hollers."

I don't know what it means either, but it somehow feels appropriate here.

The good gossip news is that this puts Tommy boy back in the game. Men love to hate Tom Cruise, rolling their eyes and calling him a girly man. Of course, this always comes from men who haven't budged from their BarcaLoungers since the Atlanta Olympics.

When they're not making headlines getting divorced and bed-hopping (see Zeta-Jones, Catherine), celebrities are always getting on silly bandwagons for this or that, and I suspect this stop-gossip foolery will have to run its course.

We have celebs to thank for a distressing recent trend called the Lesser Boyfriend. This got started with Julia Roberts and Benjamin Bratt. She is the radiant Oscar winner who is paid (notice I didn't say "earns") $25 million per movie. He is the also-ran who latched on to Julia and immediately quit his day job on *Law and Order*, where he displayed the emotional range of, say, Joe Friday.

Other celebs followed suit. J-Lo dumped Puffy Combs for an unknown backup dancer, for instance, before finally coming to her senses and discovering just what my mama always told me: it's just as easy to fall in love with a rich man as a poor one.

The lesser boyfriend? Thanks a lot, sister-chicks.

This is a trend we don't need but will no doubt trickle down and splatter all over us like so much seagull poop. I envision a nation of newly empowered men who seize this chance to become the professional wind beneath our wings.

Just sit there and look soulful while she picks up the check. Nice work if you can get it, right?

Wrong. The lesser boyfriend is a terrible idea for the Julias and the Jennifers but it's a horrendously bad idea for the Amber Dawns and Misti Raes out here in the real world, where soul boy's gonna throw in your face that he gave up his dream of becoming a professional wrassler and comic-strip artist just for you.

Of course, being a gossipmonger of the lowest order, I fed like plankton on the Big Breakup, when Julia woke up and realized she wanted somebody who could do more than anticipate the exact moment when her eight-bucks-a-bottle water was getting dangerously low in the glass.

Naturally, Bratt got married, like, six months after Julia dumped him and I'm looking at his bride and thinking: *Hell-o. You have long reddish brown hair and sausage lips. Get a clue, rebound girl.*

The point is, we can't kick gossip to the curb. Why? Because *it's fun.*

Taking a pledge to never gossip, a measure supported by this new movement, is just plain scary. The thought that I could never again speculate to all my friends and neighbors about why my mailman shaves his legs is as depressing as back fat.

That said, I do believe it's important to set the record straight if you find out you've spread misinformation. The mailman's a triathlete, it turns out, and shaves his legs to cut down on the wind resistance when he's cycling.

Yeah. I believe *that.*

2

SUVs EAT THE *Ozone?*

Hey, We All Gotta Eat Something and I Got Twenty-Seven Cup Holders

Oh, pity us poor SUV owners. No, really. Any more bad publicity and we're going to have to start meeting in church basements and drinking too much coffee before we nervously step forward to confess the awful truth: "Hi, my name is Nimrod and I drive a Ford Excursion."

"Hi, Nimrod."

Bad enough we have to pay up to $75 for a tank of gas, but now we learn that there is a national movement among la-di-da "ethics experts" to expose us as the rotten, selfish, dangerous, polluting road hogs we truly are.

These smartypants ethicists, who apparently don't find the human genome debate nearly sexy enough to ponder, believe that not nearly enough of us are "really thinking through" the decision to buy an SUV.

As one explained it, "If you buy an SUV, you're buying your safety at the expense of someone else's."

Well, yes. And your point would be?

Sorry. I know that's not the PC reaction, but let's face it. If you're driving a Hyundai, which basically runs on air and tofu, and you get in an accident with an SUV, are you going to say, "Well, at least I have the courage of my convictions"? Hell, no. You're going to say: "Soon's I get outta this hospital bed and find my legs, I'm gonna get me a Suburban. Loaded."

Why should I apologize for wanting to buy the safest family vehicle I honestly cannot afford? It's the American way.

A recent newspaper story reported that some particularly guilt-ridden potential SUV buyers are actually seeking the advice of professional "ethics consultants."

Have mercy.

These buyers are wailing and wringing their hands as they weigh the obvious benefit of owning an SUV (they're *big*) versus something smaller and weenielike (they can face themselves in the mirror—small clip-on lightless mirror that it is).

I'm guessing these flakes don't even kick the tires for fear it might hurt their feelings.

The only real advantage in owning a normal-size car is fewer trips to the gas station. Back in the day, I didn't mind pumping my own gas but that was when instructions were simpler: Remove nozzle, lift handle, pump gas, heed the siren song of the attractively displayed chocolate cream horns at the cash register, pay the man.

Today's pumps are just so irritating, carrying on little conversations on a screen: "Hi. Have a nice day. Do you wish to pay with a credit or debit card? Cash? What are you, some kind of freak? If you used the pay-at-pump card, you could just drive away without feeling forced to buy that Slurpee the size of a thirty-gallon trash can, which, between you and me, it's painfully obvious you don't need."

I despise this giant leap forward in womankind that has us pumping our own gas. Some gas pumps are so slow it's as if they've metamorphosed into eighty-year-old men with uncooperative prostates. While you fume about this, the crawl on the pump is blinking: *"Pay inside now! And don't forget the jerky!"*

Most of the attacks on the SUV come from environmentalists because, well, the emission control standards are, uh, missing.

This is sad indeed, but what can I tell you? So are my husband's.

Interestingly, most of the ethicists interviewed for the news story owned SUVs. One said he was trying not to get defensive about owning a Lincoln Navigator but added that he does have four kids. And they're really fat. (Okay, that's just a guess.)

One of the reasons I bought Bubbette was that SUVs are supposed to be so damned sturdy and dependable. To tell the truth, car maintenance isn't a priority for me. Sure, I could spend the money for an oil change or even get one of those, whatchamacallit, spare tires, but a new DVD player and blond highlights are just so much more *fun*!

I despise taking cars in for service because, sooner or later, the mechanic is going to motion me over to look under the hood.

In a way, it's endearing. He's trying very hard not to assume that I don't know coolant from Coolio, which of course I don't.

"Now, Miz Rivenbark," he'll say with tremendous earnestness, "as you can plainly see, your DPFE sensor is in dire need of replacement." He'll then point in the direction of something about the size of an Oysterette.

"It looks awfully small," I'll whine. "How much will it cost?"

The answer to this is always $165, including labor.

Doesn't matter what you have done; it's going to be $165. Just watch.

"Hey," I'll say, "can't we just skip it? I mean, I really need a root perm this week, hon."

I get the Lecture.

He starts in on emissions standards and I just watch his mouth moving, thinking that I might as well kiss the root perm *and* the tangerine ultrasuede jacket good-bye this week.

"Can't I wait a couple of months?" I ask, twirling my flat hair semiflirtatiously.

"Miz Rivenbark, you are risking *permanent damage* to the automobile," he says. "Not to mention much more costly repairs down the road."

"Oh, go ahead, then." I pout.

Of course, there's more. After an hour or so in the toxic waiting room with only an elderly *Wildlife* magazine to read and the smell of burned coffee and tires to keep me company, the mechanic returns to inform me that my automatic transmission fluid is black.

"It's my best color," I say cheerily, setting womankind back a few more decades.

"It needs *immediate replacement*," he says, practically pleading. "In fact, all your fluids are in terrible shape. Your power steering fluid and your radiator coolant are practically gummy!"

He went on, blah, blah, blah, but I was thinking about my high school years when my dad explained that you should change the oil every fifty-thousand miles or something like that. He seemed to think that was a Big Deal, so I've always been sure to at least do that part right.

I'd rather buy a new car than maintain the old one. I bought Bubbette after my midsized, fuel-efficient non-ozone-eatin' car left me stranded by the roadside. As I sat in my smoking hunk of crap on the shoulder of the interstate, hazard lights flashing (and who knew you could use them for something besides parking in the fire lane at the Food Lion to run in for milk?), I am mortified to report that not one soul stopped to help.

This is the South, for heaven's sake. Where was the concern, the hospitality, the sweet family that would, naturally, stop to offer assistance? I waved to an elderly lady who looked unlikely to hit me in the head and drag me off into the kudzu but she just gave me the finger.

If I had not had my cell phone, I would be there right now, wasting away with only a pack of Chiclets and half a hairy fruit roll-up to sustain me.

Oddly enough, just five days earlier I had joined a nationally respected automobile club, whose initials are AAA, and my shiny new temporary membership card was in my wallet.

When I called the toll-free help line, the woman on the other end of the phone sounded vaguely irritated. Why was *she* annoyed? I was late for my first big-city book signing, stressed out, and, because it was North Carolina in August, in grave danger of starting to smell like a goat.

I told her that smoke was pouring from beneath the hood of my car. I thought she might advise me to "stop, drop, and roll" or something but she seemed unimpressed. Apparently, she gets these calls all day from

Tapeworm, Alabama, to Moose Butt, Alaska, and she wasn't full of warm fuzzies.

I gave her my location, pinning it down by naming the nearest town and saying that I was approximately two miles west of it on Interstate 40. This, however, wasn't good enough.

"Ma'am," she snarled, "in the future, it is always a good idea to make a mental note of each exit you pass so that you will know exactly where you are at all times."

"What am I? Rain Man?" I snapped. "No one makes a mental note of what exit they're driving past. Six minutes till Wapner . . ."

After another testy ten minutes or so, during which time she asked everything except my shoe size and favorite brand of salsa, she asked me to describe, again, the nature of my car's problem.

"Well," I began, trying to be patient, "there's a gauge blinking red, smoke billowing out from under the hood, and an awful burning smell as if wires have all fused together into one charred mess."

There was a pause, and then she asked—and I swear I am not making this up—"Ma'am, is the vehicle driveable?"

"Sure it is," I said. "I just wanted to pull off the road and chat with you because I'm *just so frikkin' tired of arriving everywhere on time.*"

The tow truck arrived ninety minutes later, having

been given some very odd directions. Would driving an SUV have made it all better? Would the wait have been more pleasant? Perhaps not, but what can I tell you? I got twenty-seven cup holders. Life's a series of choices, hons.

3
FEELING
Squirrely

**Why Clone Cats When There's Perfectly Good Russell
Crowe Lying Around?**

My cats have gotten a whiff of the weirdest new
business around and they want in. They haven't
said anything, mind you. They are still just cats, but
they've been agitated ever since I caught them watching
a CNN report about a new cat-cloning laboratory.

I can tell they're wondering which one we'll clone.
The eleven-year-old may think he's got the edge because
we adopted him as a kitten but he scratches tic-tac-toe
games into our ankles every time we step over him and
we're, frankly, over it.

The ten-year-old is sweeter but she has only one eye
and throws up on the carpet a lot. (Then again, so does
my aunt Ollie Rae, come to think of it.)

Cloning cats is expected to be big business for the

folks at Genetic Savings and Clone (wonder if they give out free electric blankets or flatware when you open an account) who say that preserving your kitty's precious DNA is like "rescuing art from a burning building."

I've never actually owned any artwork that farts while it sleeps, but maybe that's just me.

They're working on developing the technology to clone dogs, but it's proving much more difficult because dogs have a much more complex reproductive cycle than cats.

Complex? Who are they kidding? I personally know dogs that have birthed a dozen puppies in less time than the average TNT movie commercial break.

Whatever. It's hard to understand why anybody would clone their cats when there are so many without homes already. Sure, they don't have Fluffy's sweet demeanor or Waldo's sense of wonder, but they deserve a home, not a clone.

I get the whole notion of cloning cows and sheep for medicine produced in their milk. And, hey, I wouldn't object to cloning the occasional human as long as his name was Russell Crowe, but I bet I know one person who will fight the cat-cloning business. Attorney General John Ashcroft has admitted, in front of witnesses, that he thinks cats, particularly calicos, are "evil."

Of course, this is the same guy who has doilies and

curtains placed over nude statues so he won't have to see what Archie Bunker would've called "offensible nudidity." He is wazy—way crazy, that is.

Having owned my share of calicos, I don't get it. They're no more evil than, say, tabby cats or even fluffy Persians (currently Iranians). All of them, as we know, can hack into your computer files, shred crucial Justice Department documents, and even cast spells on you that cause you to cough up some wicked hairballs during staff briefings. But other than that . . .

Of course, we're all a little loony, but shouldn't it upset the average tax-paying American to realize that the Big Justice Guy is squealing like a schoolgirl every time he sees a tricolored cat? Sure, I know they can read your mind, but even so.

And shouldn't we be concerned that Ashcroft targets the calico, which is almost always female? Isn't this further proof of what we have long suspected, that this guy really detests Estrogen Americans?

Even those with whiskers and short, pointy ears. You know, like Greta Van Susteren used to have until she had plastic surgery to become a cable news hottie.

Heaven help poor Ashcroft if he is forced to visit a museum in all his world travels. Is an advance team summoned to sprint ahead and cover any offending private parts with dish towels?

Because I firmly believe that one should confront

one's fears in order to achieve true personal growth, I suggest that Ashcroft sign up for the next celebrity *Fear Factor*. None of those sissy tricks like dangling outside a helicopter by your teeth or baby-stepping across the ledge of a skyscraper or scarfing up a plate of pig rectum. No, no. Ashcroft should be locked in a cage with a dozen or so calicos, forced to watch their evildoing: licking themselves, purring, sleeping.

Hey, don't thank me for the idea. Restoring the big guy's sanity is thanks enough.

In other news from the animal kingdom, Northwestern biologists might want to look into cloning squirrels.

Turns out there is a serious decline in the gray squirrel population in the Pacific Northwest.

I detest these rats-with-tails because they systematically hide and eat my entire pecan crop every year. During the winter months, as I step out to get my morning newspaper, they're out there waddling around my yard, patting their distended stomachs, grinning and winking at me.

The problem, according to biologists, is that boy squirrels are "eager to mate" two-thirds of the year. The other third, presumably, is reserved for football and male bonding over bowlfuls of stolen nuts. Meanwhile, girl squirrels living in rainy Washington State and perhaps suffering from SSAD (squirrel seasonal affective disorder) feel frisky for only *six hours a year*.

Unhappily for me, Southern squirrels don't have this problem. The researchers found that Southern gray squirrels, boys and girls, are pretty much "on go" all the time. As if I needed verification of that. The limbs of my two huge pecan trees are constantly swaying with the, ahem, activity of these insatiable varmints. When my daughter, then four, asked me what the squirrels were doing, I just stammered that they were "probably playing leapfrog." She said that's not how they did it in pre-school, and I said, "Thank God."

Happily, there is a solution to the lack of libido among girl squirrels in the Northwest. Biologists, concerned that the boy squirrels are "running themselves ragged trying to find a willing partner," plan to relocate the boys to remote stands of undisturbed oak and pine trees where there are said to be plenty of girl squirrels who have "lovely personalities." It's a sure bet that none of them has had a date since the Reagan years.

The whole plan has a sort of *Seven Brides for Seven Brothers* feel to it, importing menfolk to perpetuate the species. But, as a woman of the female persuasion, let me just say that these girl squirrels may need more than a new tree to get in the mood.

While I'm sure the boy squirrels will swagger into the new habitat as if they're God's gift, they should know that girls, all of us, like to be courted a bit. Perhaps an offer to help with the chores, instead of putting your squirrel feet all over the new dining table, er, nest.

Boy squirrels, try to see her as a soul mate, not just another beady-eyed conquest in a fur coat. Ask her how her day was, what her hopes and dreams are, where she hides the nuts, you get the idea.

And if things still don't go well, call your buddies on the East Coast and ask them to come out and help you. Please.

4
AND NOW A WORD
from the Cockpit . . .

"Harrummpha Lumpha Wheeee!"

According to the colorful flier that just fluttered out of my Dividend Miles statement from the airline, now you may use frequent-flier miles to go to outer space.

This seems pretty ambitious for an industry that still hasn't figured out how to serve coffee that doesn't taste like an old ashtray, but who am I to question progress?

USAirways has hit on a clever way to entice travelers who are weary of redeeming those miles for free trips to eligible cities and dates such as Poughkeepsie in midwinter (Saturday night stay required; subject to capacity controls and blackouts, dealer taxes and tags extra, 8:00 P.M., 7:00 Central).

By partnering with SpaceAdventures, the company that has made a fortune shuttling bored Thurston Howell

III types to the International Space Station, the airline is offering regular jugheads like you and me the chance to, among other choices, "accelerate faster than the speed of sound in a MiG-25 fighter jet and see the curvature of the earth below." Of course, in my case the view would be obstructed by my breakfast all over the windshield, but no matter.

Another trip offered by the airline will allow you to "float weightlessly just like the astronauts in a plane departing from the Yuri Gagarin Cosmonaut Training Center in Russia," which, I believe, is conveniently located between the Yuri Gagarin Stop 'n' Rob and the Yuri Gagarin Eyeglasses-in-an-Hour Stand.

Traveling into outer space with the airlines in charge could still be a bit dicey.

The only thing worse than being seated beside some Jabba on a cross-country flight would be going into space beside him so he has even more time to nag you for the rest of your string cheese.

Especially in light of the terrorism attacks, it's unbelievable to me that there are still some people who are obnoxious on airplanes.

I adore the thought of federal marshals being onboard, though I'm puzzled why they must sit in first class, bogarting the hot fudge sundaes and heated towels. I mean, it is supposed to be a job, isn't it? We paying passengers are sitting back here in the crates-of-live-poultry class, eating brick-hard pastries that taste like they were baked in somebody's Queasy Bake oven.

Still, we need extra protection when there are idiots like the West Coast passenger I read about recently who sparked a brawl and injured four passengers. Nobody said why he got so mad, but I suspect it was because he discovered that he paid $2,350.69 for his round-trip ticket, and the guy beside him paid about $17.50 plus tax. While that is a maddening little airline habit, this is no time for picking a fight on an airplane.

Where does this guy get off? If I was the captain, the answer to that question would be "somewhere around Phoenix," via a handy-dandy, anti-terrorism, anti-asshole Rowdy Passengers Trapdoor System (the RP-TS, in airline lingo).

All you'd have to do is lure the loser to the secret trapdoor spot, pull a lever, and, quick as the other passengers could circle around and chant "See ya, wouldn't wanna be ya!" that little problem in 12-C would have frosty eyelashes and a buttload of regrets.

There are other problems with outer-space travel via commercial airlines. For starters, your fellow space passengers will probably try to cram even more luggage into the overhead compartment because who knows what the weather's like up there and you know there's always that one loser who has to pack skis and a crate of lobsters.

While we're on that subject, let me just say how much I admire flight attendants. I have seen them take a six-foot duffle bag, stomp it down to the size of a stick of Dentyne, and then look around like "What's your problem, fool?" We are not worthy.

And people, please. Let's all check a few bags, shall we? I mean, not me, of course, but the rest of you. I do my part, after all. When I used to fly with my toddler, she was kept where all crying, unruly children should be kept, safely stowed in the overhead compartment. With all the lobsters up there, it wasn't like she was gonna starve, now, was it?

Frankly, it seems to me that we ought to get a few things straight in our own atmosphere before we start flying into outer space.

On a recent flight I was treated to the usual spellbinding demonstration of how to buckle a seat belt and the usual "if the oxygen mask drops and you're with a small child, put yours on first" spiel. Sure, it makes sense in the big picture but don't you think you'd feel just a smidgen guilty if that mask, which looks like a sinister yellow puppet screaming *we're all gonna die*, dropped down and you put it on first while your kid sat there watching *Stuart Little 2* and trying to breathe? Sure you would.

The thing that throws me every time I fly is how airlines expect us to feel relaxed about flying even though the pilot's microphone doesn't even work. It's hard to feel confident when your kid's Junior Karaoke machine from K-Tel has better sound quality, am I right?

So you're flying at 35,000 feet or so and the pilot—you think—is saying something about "reaching cruising altitude" but you're not sure because every other word doesn't come out. You hear, "Good morning, folks, from deck...skies...wind...miles...hour...cruising...Grand Canyon . . . she looked like she was eighteen . . . Hey! Is that smoke?"

At least, through it all, the airlines have a sense of humor. How else do you explain the warning on the back of every seat: "Please fasten seat belt while seated"? Try doing it standing. I can tell you it's damn near impossible.

And they love to switch your gate at the last minute, just for kicks. ("Cincinnati? Oh yes, that flight will depart from gate C-four.") You turn, walk away, and imagine a snicker, then a chorus of guffaws as you get farther away. At C-4, sure enough, you've been bounced to B-14. Gotcha!

And don't fall for that business about the flight being delayed because of "problems with inbound equipment." This is airlinespeak for "broken airplane."

Overall, however, I think outer-space travel with frequent-flier points has definite appeal.

For instance, let's say you've got one of those "The

Thing That Wouldn't Leave" relatives staying at your house. Just boot 'em into orbit. ("You'll love Jupiter, Aunt Tootie. Hmmm? Oxygen? No, I don't believe they need that sort of thing up there. Buh-bye, now.")

The brochure promises that the new program allows the airline to "take you where no other airline has gone before." It's a nice thought but how about we settle for getting off the Tarmac in under an hour?

It's not like I'm asking for the moon, you know.

5

THIS JUST IN
from the Workplace

Everything Still Sucks

Every now and then, I like to share some solid, sensible advice with young people who are thinking about getting a summer job. This is important because— and I'm sure we all agree—today's young people are tomorrow's old people and our nation's children are our greatest natural resource. Well. Along with that cool new striped ketchup.

Having had a few summer jobs in my own teenhood, allow me to explain, my young friends, How to Dress for a Summer Job Interview.

For starters, you will want to avoid wearing any T-shirt that appears to be stained, torn, faded, or reads Beauty Is in the Eye of the Beer Holder.

While this is admittedly hilarious, it is doubtful that your prospective employer will get the joke. Most prospective employers pride themselves on being Serious Types, who will remind you that they are not paying you to be funny. Unless, of course, you're me. Ha!

Young people, aside from dressing sensibly, you should also take great pains to check your vocabulary, avoiding the popular job applicant pitfall of lapsing into teenage slang. This slang will only confuse/scare your potential employer. Here is an example:

CORRECT: "I want to become a valued member of the Widgetville team!"

INCORRECT: "That weird machinery sound coming from over there is harshing my mellow, playa."

Now seems a good time to mention that you should always remember that, no matter what summer job you end up with, The Customer Is Always Right.

No, really, I'm serious. The customer can basically treat you any way he or she wants and you must remain courteous and helpful. As in: "May I please show you the way to the exit door, you rotting corn pad of a human being?"

Once you are secure in your new job, my young friends, you must avoid the temptation to engage in what is commonly known as "white collar crime." This dastardly practice occurs when workers take home office supplies, etc., rationalizing that no one will miss packs of pens or notepads or the random laptop or three that can be sold on eBay.

I understand the temptation. Let's just say that during a brief period in the mid-1970s, customers at a certain seafood restaurant never really got the forty-shrimp "barge" as ordered because five to ten of those suckers would mysteriously topple off the barge and into my mouth. Then again, what kind of a lard-ass orders anything called a barge? Talk about a cry for help.

Finally, don't ever talk back to your boss if you expect to keep your summer job.

CORRECT: "I'm sorry I was late, sir. In the future, I will check the schedule for possible last-minute changes!"

INCORRECT: "Yeah, right. Next time, I'll be sure to look in the sky for the frikkin' bat signal to tell me you buttholes have changed my shift again."

I don't want to limit my helpful advice to teenagers, of course. Let's see what we can do to help those unemployed dot-com'ers out there circling the want ads at their mommy's kitchen table and wondering why they ever bought that silly Mercedes Benz SUV (Billy Bob meets the snooty Grey Poupon dude; what *is* that?).

I don't wish unemployment on anyone, except perhaps Eminem, so now seems a good time for some résumé-polishing advice.

A lot of downsized techno types like to post their résumés on the Internet where they can be assured that it will not be ignored by dozens of human resources managers but rather will be ignored by many thousands of human resources managers across this great land of ours.

The truth is, nobody gets a Real Job unless they know somebody. It has never happened in the history of job-gettingdom. Just ask Melissa Rivers. It's just like the experts say, location, location, location. No, wrong, experts. It's not what you know, it's who you know. Like if you know someone who has photos of the boss doing the nasty with the chick who changes the toner in the copying machine once a month, your job future is rosy indeed.

If blackmail is repulsive to you, take the high road and get a job the old-fashioned way: Stalking. Try to make friends with somebody who works high up in the company where you're looking. Hang out at the gym where they work out, manage to dine one table over at their favorite restaurant, shop in the same stores.

After a few weeks of this, you will either (1) have made small talk and a new friend who is dazzled by your knowledge and experience or (2) have Mr. Restraining Order filed against you.

Here's some more advice. You dot-com types just love Web sites and we know you're just dying to "link" your résumé to your Web site. This isn't a bad idea if your Web site is a lively, well-written look into your professional soul.

However, most of you people who have your own Web sites tend to think the whole world will find it pee-on-yourself funny to see photos of you in your college days, face painted and the words UNC Sucks scrawled across your bare belly at the Big Game. Take care that your Web site is free of such drivel as photos of you romping with your new chocolate lab (no one cares) or your fiancée and you looking happily drenched during a rousing afternoon of whitewater rafting (bring back the dog pictures).

A final note of caution: On the off chance that somebody actually does slip up and call you to come in for an interview, your telephone answering machine message should always be crisp and professional.

WRONG: "I'm just a love machine, oooooh baby, I'm just a love machine, and I won't work for nobody but you, oooh, baby. . . ."

ALSO WRONG: "Hi, you've reached Ted and Susan's answering machine. We are currently screening our calls because *you people make us sick!*"

WRONGEST OF ALL: (Sound of heavily congested toddler mouthbreathing into the phone for several seconds, then): "Mommy and Daddy not home. Please moofully moofala." (sound of phone crashing to floor and loud wailing) *Beeeep*.

Remember, dot-com'ers, a man who builds his future on shifting sands or nonexistent companies making nonexistent products is doomed to repeat himself.

Okay, so let's pretend you now have a job—a real one. You'll need to brush up on your business-speak. Practice saying things like: "Let's take a meeting, do lunch, my girl calls your girl. Let's download on one another (unless one of us is a pigeon, of course). Let's interface, reconnect, get up to speed, on the same page, touch base.

"You're in my tickle file so I'm going to pick your brain. (Hold still. Wouldn't want to lose your sense of smell!) Now we're playing phone tag, our eyes on the prize, our ears to the ground, our backs to the wall, our butts on our shoulders, whatever."

Now, I agree that business-speak can be as annoying as a Mr. T comeback, but if you're going to run with the wolves, go with the flow, grow the company, you better know the lingo.

You'll also need to get reacquainted with the Weekly Staff Meeting. Personally, I'd rather spend a couple of hundred hours bikini waxing Robin Williams than go to one, but this is about you, not me.

I've been to tons of newspaper staff meetings over the years and no one has ever figured out how to make them interesting, although I did have fun one time making out with my almost-husband during a slide show on bloodborne pathogens in the workplace.

The fact is, you can't run a big, successful, or even a little, piddling company without meetings. You simply can't run a successful organization unless you, once a week, systematically herd your employees into a small room that smells vaguely like ass where all the employees can do is look at the bad hotel art on the walls and imagine what the boss looks like nekkid.

You stop having staff meetings and, next thing you know, we'll see the collapse of the entire U.S. economy. Oops. Too late.

Staff meetings are always long because, in every organization, there is one flunkie-lackey-minion-toadie who loves the sound of his own voice.

He's the one who leans forward at the end of the meeting, pen raised in the air, and says, "Just one more thing, Chief . . ."

I'm not sure what motivates these freaks but I do know that, by the time you finally get out of the meeting, your clothes are out of style.

You can avoid so much of this silliness if you follow my example and work at home.

For years, I've worked at home in (fall/winter) dorm pants and sweatshirt or (spring/summer) sports bra and Joe Boxer shorts.

But all that's going to change because I just read an article that says that "not dressing for work just because no one's going to see you sends the wrong message."

The article got me so worked up I fired a nasty memo to myself and demanded that I shape up immediately.

The article said that wearing PJs or loungewear while "working" could "influence the quality of your work and your relationship with your clients."

I'm going to dress more professionally at home, even though the whole thing smacks of the jealous rantings of someone pinned more tightly than a prom-night orchid to a windowless office in some nameless bank-building minicity.

And for those of you who don't work at home but do have a Casual Friday, where you get to dress down a bit, always remember (men), No Velcro, and (women), if Pamela Anderson would wear it, y'all just don't.

6

TV OR
Not TV

Oh, It's Never a Question in My House

I have a close friend who refuses to buy a television. Her two children are slowly going blind watching DVD movies on their tiny laptop computers, which for some reason is okay, but she and her husband are standing firm. No TV. It only creates a rotting cabbage pile of brain cells that, otherwise, would've developed into fabulous, fluffy cells ready to take on cures for cancer, Renaissance-quality art, the Great American Novel, or, just dreaming here, a plastic wrap that won't stick to itself and leave you throwing it against the wall and crying on the floor surrounded by naked sandwiches.

They have a media room in their new home, and it is lovely except for the black hole where the TV should be.

No TV, they say in that unmistakably I'm-smarter-than-*you*-are singsong so favored by their kind.

Now, far be it from me to point out the threat of impending macular degeneration on the tots downstairs in one of the nonmedia rooms as they strain and tilt to get a better view of *Spider-Man*, the inch-tall version.

To each his own, I always say. Well. Not really. Actually I never say that. I'm hooked on TV, unapologetically, unregretfully, unabashedly. Sure, there's some stinky stuff on TV, but, hey, there are crappy books, too, am I right?

I'm forever telling my friend about all the great shows she's missing, and she's forever telling me that she is very, very worried about me. Believe me, if I had it to do over again, I'd never have told her that if I had a boy, we were going to name him Cable.

It's just that I can't understand how anyone can get through the week without *Iron Chef* or *Trading Spaces*.

For those of you who haven't seen *Iron Chef*, let me explain, my dear "clueless-san." Four top chefs from Japan compete with a challenger, preparing elaborate multicourse meals using a preselected ingredient (often something that looks as if it came off the bottom of someone's shoe and frequently still wriggling a bit). The dishes, all prepared in one hour, are then judged by a Japanese panel that includes a politician who has never met a cup of sake he didn't like, a waiflike actress, a snooty fortune-teller, and some actor. The show is in Japanese so it's dubbed, and painfully so. *"Watakushi no kioku ga tashika naraba"* then becomes simply "Yep."

Japanese think we all talk like John Wayne or Sheriff Buford Pusser. They always dub in answers like "Yep," "Nope," or "I shoulda shot you when I had the chance, pilgrim."

For truly crazed fans, there's even an *Iron Chef* drinking game in which viewers down a beer each time the show's creator, "Chairman" Takeshi Kata, says *"Allez cuisine!"* ("To the kitchen!") or anytime the ubiquitous birdlike actress takes a bite during the judging segment, flutters nervously, and says, "Oh! I feel an explosion in my mouth!" The way she says it, I'm fairly convinced she's no stranger to porn.

The cult following for *Iron Chef* is huge, perhaps because of the campy Kaga, who wears Elvis hair and lacy capes with ruffly gloves and looks like some nice Asian family's flaming cousin that they're not allowed to talk about anymore.

At Kaga's command, the four Iron Chefs rise to the rafters on hydraulic pedestals. Just like I'm sure y'all do every time it's time to make the meat loaf.

Kaga then announces the ingredient, which is lowered from the ceiling, I kid you not, and never resembles anything in the all-American pantry. Stuff like natto (fermented soybean mush), lotus leaves, and octopus eyes, all of which will very likely be turned into some kind of sorbet during the dessert portion. The Japanese are very big on sorbet, even if it winks back.

The Iron Chefs are especially snippy when facing an American challenger. In a recent episode, play-by-play announcer Ota Shinichiro sniffed at "the American from San Franceesco" who couldn't possibly know anything about fresh seafood.

Sure, homeboy was used to dealing with grouper and mahi more than steroidal sardines and six-foot-long eels, but he won and I was proud to be an American. Yep, I was.

Trading Spaces is equally addictive. The premise is simple: armed with a budget of one thousand dollars, a designer, and carpenter, neighbors redo one room in each other's house. Neither couple is allowed to see what's going on in their home until time's up, forty-eight hours later.

Can you say train wreck?

I've only seen one or two participants burst into tears when shown the "new" room, but there's always that delicious tension as the details sink in.

The show's designers are young, hip, and relentlessly cheerful. One thing I've learned from watching *Trading Spaces* is that all designers hate ceiling fans. They'd rather see you install life-size ceramic spaniels wearing glue-on eyelashes on either side of your fireplace.

Letting the neighbors decorate your house is scary, or

not, depending on where you live. ("Melba, what we need with a laundry room when we got a perfectly good front porch?")

I've had some neighbors that I wouldn't trust to decorate a goldfish bowl. And what if you find out, too late, that they're just doing this to get even with you for tossing their dog's poop back into their yard. Well. On their front steps, actually.

Even if your neighbors are delightful people of taste, it's still kind of creepy to think about them pawing through your things, tossing out your antique rice bed and botanical prints and replacing them with painted dollar-store pillows, some sad homemade futon, and framed magazine covers, all in the name of "freshening up!"

Just once I'd love to see the neighbors come to blows. Call it X-treme decorating. Let's be honest. In the case of the couple who stenciled purple harlequins on their neighbors' living room walls, I'm thinking that the classic "But Your Honor, they needed killin' " defense might just work.

Although I love the show, I'll never be able to participate because my hubby and I aren't handy. The *Trading Spaces* couples are all nauseatingly competent. If the designer says, "We've got an hour! Go stuff and sew seven bolster pillows and hand-paint a scroll pattern on all the furniture!" they just smile and say upbeat Midwestern things like, "Righty-o!" or "We're on it!" We'd just stare blankly and say, "Do who?"

Trading Spaces is part of the reality-TV trend which includes *The Osboumes*, a surprisingly appealing look into the domestic life of bathead-eating rocker Ozzy Osbourne, his supportive foulmouthed wife, and spoiled, foulmouthed teenagers.

There's something enormously appealing about watching Ozzy take his trash out. We're mystified that rich people take their own trash out and Ozzy, in turn, is puzzled that we would think he has "a @#$% trash roadie."

Although I admit to loving Ozzy, things have gotten ridiculous when Anna Nicole Smith gets her own reality-TV series. Not to mention planned shows starring the poutsome Sean P. Diddy Combs, who hasn't stopped nagging MTV for his own show ever since he saw Ozzy's Nielsens. VH-1 fortunately wriggled out of a deal to film newlyweds Liza Minnelli and David Gest whose marriage lasted slightly longer than a cough drop.

Kiss frontman Gene Simmons is pitching a show about his life but I don't hold out much hope for it. How many times can he brush his teeth and show us his famous tongue in a single thirty-minute episode?

Even "actress" Cybill Shepherd is begging for cameras to be installed in her home. No, thanks. I think I have to wash my hair that night.

Face it. Not everybody's life is worth watching. I don't

want to see a reality-TV show about Ashley Judd, who men love because she looks that great *and* can make a pan of homemade biscuits for her man in the time it takes for you to say, "Well, shouldn't she just be taken out and *shot*?"

And spare me *Life with Naomi Campbell* in which the supermodel lounges about in patched jeans and a T-shirt that reads Like a Virgin. Guess her The Drunker I Get, the Better You Look shirt was still at the cleaners.

But back to Liza, whose ill-fated Big Fat Geek Wedding should have satisfied her PR jones for a while. Now in divorce court, Liza's probably relieved that VH-1 nixed plans to film her and Gest as they sat around Caesar's penthouse counting their money between plastic surgery appointments. Let's face it; if this guy gets any more brow lifts, he's going to have eyes in the back of his head for real.

I'm not picking on the rich and famous. The fact is poor and middle-class folks are often boring, too. You don't see me lobbying the networks for a reality show on my life, do you? It wouldn't exactly be a ratings bonanza.

Typical day?

7:30 A.M.: Stumble into kitchen, eat Fruity Pebbles from the box; read paper in jammies; pack lunch for hubby; clean up cat throw-up; drink *lots* of coffee.

Noon: Stumble into kitchen, fix lunch for five-year-old, who announces she's "booooorrrreeeed" despite morning summer camp that included simulated "croc wrestling" and construction of realistic log fort. Watch (you guessed it) *Days of Our Lives* while ironing hubby's shirts. Get through half a shirt before abandoning project to devote full attention to sexy new character, Tony Di-Mera.

3:00 P.M.–6:00 P.M.: Make appointment to have tires rotated, clean up cat throw-up (again), play eight games of Chutes and Ladders *until I win,* deliver shirts to dry cleaners because "I don't have to live like this," inform pesky telemarketer that I can't afford a home security system unless I sell another kidney.

6:30 P.M.–7:00 P.M.: Write enticing newspaper ad offering free cat to "just so-so home."

9:00 P.M.–10:00 P.M.: Read stories and sing songs to five-year-old, who refuses to go to sleep because she's excited having "just made a poopie the size of a ham."

Midnight: Wake up in child's bed clutching copy of *Oh Say Can You Seed?*

Yeah, I'm not quite ready for TV yet. I just like to watch.

My TV-hating friend does enjoy going to movies and we've spent the summer taking our tots to a bunch of them, the lure of a dark, cold theater and a frosty, five-dollar Coke proving irrationally powerful.

That said, we have been grappling with the mommy moral dilemma: Is it ever okay to tank the kiddies up on fruit roll-ups and "buttered" popcorn, kiss their noggins, and sneak next door to watch a grown-up movie?

As I sat beside my daughter and her friends watching *Spirit: Stallion of the Cimarron* and feeling like "Mommy: Resentful of Formulaic Kid Movies with Dubious Heroes," I realized I might be on kid-movie overload.

After all, everybody gushes about this movie about a handsome animated horse that wants to roam free instead of live in a sixth-floor walkup like his horse buddies in the city. Actually, it's about the Evil Railroad coming through the West and how one mythical horse managed to blow up enough buildings, railroad tracks, and people to stop Progress. I believe I was the only person in the crowded theater who thought it was sad that all the railroad workers got blown to kingdom come, being silly expendable humans, while the horses were free at last, free at last. (A romantic subplot had Cimarron fall for a pretty girl horse who, you guessed it, turned out to be a nag.)

We went to *Lilo & Stitch* next, a Disney movie with a hero (Stitch) that looks a lot like that thing that burst out of Sigourney Weaver's chest so many years ago, only it's blue. Lilo is a plump, disliked Hawaiian child who makes friends with alien Stitch, who is posing as a plump, disliked Hawaiian dog. I hated 'em both.

I did like Lilo's older sister (and kudos to Disney for

finally drawing a heroine who is pretty *and* has enormous thighs) who is hassled by Child Protective Services for leaving the bratsome Lilo home alone with power tools and aliens and such. I'm thinking, who could blame her?

My friend without the TV says she's not too worried about her kids missing *Spy Kids 2* because it will be available on DVD soon, anyway.

Y'all pray for their little eyeballs.

7

CIRRUS, SCHMIRRUS...
They're All Just Puffy to Me

My friend Lisa Marie turned me on to the video trivia games at a local wings-and-beer restaurant and I haven't been the same since.

Quick! Where in the body would you find the dura mater? The heart, lungs, bottom of the feet, circulatory system, or skull?

Lisa guessed right (skull) and got one thousand points; me? I got zero, zip, nada, goose egg.

Quick again! Before *Thirtysomething*, actor Timothy Busfield starred as a doctor's stepson on which medical drama? *Quincy; St. Elsewhere; Trapper John, MD; Emergency;* or *Medical Center*?

Lisa Marie smugly punched the number for *Trapper John*. Did I imagine it or did she appear to be shielding her answer from me? I guessed *Quincy* but when she won another one thousand points, I pathetically asked her if she recalled that Chad Everett had starred in *Medical Center* back in the '80s.

"It was the seventies," she said, dismissing me with a wave and readjusting her librarian-ass glasses. Okay, I was starting to get bitter.

The geography "brain-buster" round was supremely embarrassing for me. I'd never gotten beyond the fourth-grade geography class in which Rosalita and Pedro baked tamales on an outdoor heated stone somewhere in South America. Unless the next question was going to be about my mythical nine-year-old friends wearing their gaily colored serapes, forget it.

While Lisa Marie's tally climbed for all the world—or, okay, just this particular 5,500 square feet of it—to see, I regretted the hubris I had shown by using my real name for the five-letter "screen name" that would be flashed overhead on ten different monitors. There was my name, everywhere, with a big fat "0" beside it. I should have opted for "l-o-s-e-r."

Lisa Marie was on fire, and not just from the jalapeño poppers. She was fighting it out for the top spot with a guy she recognized as a regular and seated at the bar.

"He comes here every night," she said with a sneer.

"Lisa Marie, for God's sake, the man is in a wheelchair," I said.

"His brain isn't handicapped," she snapped. "Just look at his score."

"He's handi-capable," I said. "They don't like to be called handicapped anymore."

"Oh, screw that PC stuff," Lisa Marie said. "You only have two minutes to pee between games. Be right back."

She stood up, kicked her chair back, sprinted toward the ladies' room, and, when she thought I wasn't looking, gave the finger to the guy in the wheelchair.

She returned in what must've been some kind of Woman's World Potty Record, about forty-five seconds, and informed me that she'd learned how to pee standing up just for occasions such as this.

"Anybody can do it," she said, "it just takes a little practice."

Who was this woman? And what was going on inside her dura mater?

Once settled, Lisa Marie resumed scowling at the only person keeping her from an uncontested number-one ranking.

"He's here every damn night," she said again with that poor-thing-he-has-no-life tone in her voice.

"Oh yeah?" I mustered, suddenly feeling like the brain-iac. "How do *you* know?"

It was a real Perry Mason moment, I swear. And, yes, Raymond Burr played Perry way before he went on to star (in a wheelchair!) in *Ironsides* with Don Galloway and, uh, Barbara something-or-other. So where were those kinds of questions? Huh? I can't *hear* you.

Lisa Marie didn't answer me because she was already demonstrating her fast-fingers prowess by punching in the correct answer to a question about which fish actually exists: brainfish, kidneyfish, liverfish, lungfish, or thumbfish. She selected "lungfish" while I went for the obviously correct "brainfish."

"They call it brain food for a reason," I chided her, as we waited for the correct answer to flash on the wide screen.

"Looks like you better tank up on some more," she said, as "lungfish" appeared overhead in huge letters.

Lisa Marie's total climbed into six figures. I was one cooked tamale.

At last, I got on the board by knowing that Winona Ryder's real last name was Horowitz but it was too little, too late. Lisa Marie knew the difference between "stratus" and "cirrus" clouds. All this time, I just thought they were all "puffy."

Ever since Lisa Marie kicked my ass at trivia, I've gone back at least once a week to play the game. I've learned that it's more fun if you make it a point to play with really stupid people. Like Trent Lott. Sadly, Trent's usually busy, plus he's forever trying to get me to listen to the latest MP3 from Pusha T and Malice while I'm trying to play.

"It's blackalicious!" Trent's always telling me as we share a basket of jerk-sauce wings, not surprisingly his favorite flavor, while he just goes on and on and on about the importance of reparations to the descendants of slaves.

Okay, I made that part up. Trent Lott and I have never technically shared anything except, perhaps, an irrational fondness for big hair.

After all this practice, I'm still not very good at trivia, or peeing standing up, but I'm strangely hooked. Like a lungfish.

8

I AM BOOBALICIOUS,
Hear Me Roar

How Computer Hackers Ruined My Rep

I've had a stressful week ever since some evil, smelly little computer hacker got my password and started sending some frighteningly nasty porn to everyone in my address book.

In my screen name.

Sadly, I've heard from at least a half dozen pervs across this great nation who say they sure did enjoy what "I" sent them (signing off as "Boobalicious" no less) and wondering where they can download some more.

Well I never.

I am a Methodist Sunday school teacher, for heaven's sake, the mama of a small innocent child. I do not spend my nights downloading files to strangers describing my stupendous ta-tas. Anybody who knows me personally would realize that I can barely scrape up a "ta," so that's just crazy.

No, Mr. Porn Creep Hacker, I spend my spare time tinting icing red so I can make twenty graham cracker "fire trucks" complete with ladders made of pretzel sticks and tires made of Oreos, for my daughter's kindergarten class. It is Fire Safety Week, you know. Asshole.

So, do not write me! I am *not* Boobalicious, the "randy woman from Carolina" that you think I am. As Aunt Neecie said after she foolishly answered the front door wearing only her pantyhose, I am "prostate with embarrassment."

I wouldn't have known anything about this except my Internet service provider revoked my password and cut me off from the world, saying, in so many words, that I was making them sick.

This was not the first time my computer has reprimanded me. Sometimes, it yells that I have performed an "illegal operation," which makes it sound as if I'm sharpening rusty scalpels for a back-alley abortion somewhere. Sometimes I resort to the nontechie's solution to the frozen computer, shared with me, Yoda style, by the aging, big-eared systems guru at my old newspaper. When all else would fail, he would start out, solemnly, "You must this remember . . ."

"Yes? Yes?" I said, eagerly. This man was, you should

understand, a computer wizard of the highest order. He could coax a virus out of an entire newsroom's worth of PCs simply by laying his tiny, misshapen hands on the screen.

The wisdom he would impart would be something I would cherish until the end of time.

"Tell me. What should I do?"

"Yes, child. Patient you must be."

"Tell me! What should I do?"

"Oh, okay. Are you ready?"

"Yes! Yes!"

"Just unplug the sonovabitch."

So, whenever my screen freezes or pouts or gets generally pissy, I just follow those words and things get back to normal.

Of course, there's the inevitable lecture when I plug it back in, lots of drivel about how I shut the system down "improperly." I'm fully expecting it to one day add, "Hey! Did you just unplug the sonovabitch, and don't even *think* about lying to me."

After the on-screen tongue-lashing, the computer then makes (or so I think) an elaborate sighing noise and, very slowly just to torment me, begins the process of checking the various systems to see if there is any "lost data." It's a game we play. It knows perfectly well I unplugged the sonovabitch but it has to act like it doesn't know.

The churlish messages continue, stopping just short of accusing me of drinking milk from the carton and never calling my parents.

The whole Boobalicious thing was embarrassing because I had to explain, in an overkill, protesting-too-much message to friends that I would never, ever send them porn, blah, blah, blah.

Shortly after service was restored and Boobalicious disappeared mercifully into banished-whore cyberspace, my computer contracted some sort of "worm" virus. It absolutely amazes me that these viruses, which can cripple an entire Fortune 500 company, usually originate in the darkened bedroom of some bored teenager who logs off after mom calls him to dinner and, oh boy, it's taco night!

I had to call in a professional to kill the worm. Two hours and $250 later, I was pronounced virus free and was warned never to open an e-mail from someone I don't know.

That won't be a problem because I never open half the e-mail I get from folks I do know. That's because many of my friends are compulsive forwarders.

It is beyond all understanding why anyone thinks I want to read these lame jokes or "heartwarming" stories that fairly gum up my keyboard with treacle.

A lot of it is just outright nutty, like the one about "This young Peruvian boy who was born without a tongue and was able to survive by drinking yak's milk and eating a paste made of rotted figs and mayonnaise, and, well, that young boy, ladies and gentlemen is (sniff, sniff) Mr. Julio Iglesias!"

It's a lot of stuff like you read in those Chicken Soup books, more of that develop a soul in less time that it takes to find out that—surprise!—Jiffy Lube thinks your air filter needs replacing. (True story: My friend asked her husband for one of those for Mother's Day and he bought her an actual cookbook filled with recipes for chicken soup. Here's a thought: *Chicken Soup for the Person Who Really Just Wants a Chicken Soup Cookbook.*)

Not all e-mail forwards are bad, of course. Just like all chain letters aren't bad. Right now, I'm waiting to receive my *fifty thousand U.S. dollars* after mailing letters to seven lucky friends last week. Hey, I'd have to be some kind of a mo-ron to pass on the chance to make that kind of money.

Maybe the biggest reason I detest forwards, aside from the fact that they are so damned impersonal, reducing you to line 32 of a list of "friends" that includes the sender's florist and dentist, is that I am not smart enough to know how to send one myself.

I am a computer illiterate, so nothing, short of paragraph indentions, comes easy. When my husband told me that I could type in italics by typing "control" and then the letter *I*, I *couldn't believe it!!!!* I started italicizing everything until he told me about "control" and *B* and **you can just imagine what happened next!**

My five-year-old is far more at home at the keyboard than me and I know that's just one more smidgen of evidence that my generation is just circling the drain. That, plus I heard myself tell my husband that it was "high time that we bought a rain gauge" the other day.

I've also heard myself joining the old folks in wondering why, if you call the phone company, the cable company, etc., you can't "talk to a real live human being."

Just this week, the phone company's vast computer system toyed with me through several levels of pressing 1, 2, buckle my shoe, and so on, before informing me that "The number you have dialed is no longer in service. Please hang up and try again."

"No longer in service! *You're the phone company!*" I screeched to a recording.

Smugly, I dialed the repair number and managed to navigate the phone tree forest to the department I needed. But my rush of accomplishment evaporated after too many minutes of horrendous Muzak that included Neil Diamond's "I Am, I Said," widely regarded as *the worst song ever written* as we wonder, once again, why Neil is puzzled that "no one heard, not even the chair."

I gave up and called back that night and was told by a pinched, computer-generated voice that "If you continue to hold, your call will be answered in eight minutes." I don't want to say this was wildly inaccurate, but by the time I finally got connected, my legs needed shaving again.

Repeatedly, a perky automated voice checked in to remind me that my patience (ha!) was appreciated and that my call was *very* important to everyone in the entire organization. (Ha-ha!) Screw them. I just knew that we were all on hold while they were at some club pounding apple martinis and laughing their butts off at all of us idiots on hold across America.

Coming full circle, sorta, I realized that I should try doing all this stuff via computer. Sure, cyberspace had done me wrong, but maybe this was one case where the Internet could be my friend. For all I knew, I was one of a thousand computer-phobic losers on hold out there.

I logged on to the phone company's Web site, clicked on "new service request," and watched things proceed quickly and efficiently. This was fabulous! I could fairly smell the new phone number I needed when, suddenly, the screen blared that it couldn't process my request because *"your address does not exist."* I shall share this at tax time, believe me. House? What house?

I decided to try changing my cable service the same week because as long as you're trying to gouge your eyes out, you might as well do a twofer.

On hold for forty-five minutes with more schizophrenic, computer-generated Muzak selections, it was like having Sybil as a DJ. First rockabilly, then classical, then Manilow, then gangsta rap. I was told, every twenty seconds or so, that "all of our representatives are assisting other customers." I was seized with an irrational hatred of these "other customers." Who were they and what made them so frikkin' special?

I finally got very helpful humans at both the phone and cable company but the cost to my sanity was great. Isn't that right, chair?

9

SILLY LAWSUITS COULD
Clog a Toto

Or, How My Trash Cart Nearly Killed Me

Just how dumb do manufacturers think we consumers are? Consider the instructions that came with my new hair dryer: "Do not use this product while taking a bath or shower." Shoot. It's such a time saver except for those pesky third-degree burns.

Or consider the instructions on my favorite frozen pizza: "Do not eat pizza without cooking." ("Break me off another chunk of pepperoni, Pearlie Ray, and get the broom; that dadgum cheese is scattering everywhere again.")

The box also recommends that you "remove pizza from box before cooking." Ummm. Nothing says lovin' like the smell of burning cardboard in the oven to some folks, I guess.

Here's what else I found around the house:

On a bottle of bleach: "Do not drink." (Sure, you'll have whiter, brighter insides but it won't much matter, where you're going.)

On the oven: "Do not attempt to replace oven bulb while oven is in use."

On the hot water heater: "If building in which heater resides is on fire, do not go into building."

On the dishwasher: "Remove bones and large pieces of food before placing dish in dishwasher." (Sure, the turkey carcass will never be truly clean, but do we really care?)

On the ceiling fan: "Do not place foreign objects between fan blades while fan is in motion."

On a Barney game: "Never leave Actimates Barney in the rain or snow." (Unless, like me, you can't stomach one more "Super-dee-duper!" when you step on him in the dark.)

On the VCR: "Do not use this product in the rain." (Okay, couch, chair, and love seat, everybody *back* into the living room.)

And my favorite, which wins points for creativity of expression, comes from the manual for my kid's bike helmet: "Helmets can't prevent damage from shaking, just as an egg can be completely scrambled inside its shell just by shaking it." (Gruesome, but memorable. Plus I think we've all learned a fun new way to prepare scrambled eggs.) Also from that manual: "Do not wear helmet on playground or while climbing trees." (Unless, of course, you are in the running for the coveted Nerd of the Year Award at your elementary school.)

Now I am fully aware that the reason for these warnings is that some idiot somewhere has done everything listed so the manufacturer, in hopes of avoiding Mr. Frivolous Lawsuit, has to spell it out.

Americans sue each other over everything. Look no further for proof that something is terribly wrong with our judicial system when a fat guy can sue McDonald's, Wendy's, Burger King, and KFC for making him unhealthy.

Caesar Barber, a New York maintenance worker who weighs 272 pounds and has eaten fast food for five decades, claimed in a lawsuit filed recently that he had no idea the food wasn't healthy.

Oh, hail Caesar. You gotta be kidding.

This is as wacky as those eight-hundred-pound freaks who dress in bedsheets and wail to the skinny guy making the documentary that they can't hardly get out of bed in the morning after eating a couple of dozen eggs and a case of Moon Pies for breakfast.

You reckon?

Fast food is what it is: fatty, full of salt, and fried or grilled in a puddle of grease. And that's just the salads.

Look, I love fast food. If you cut me open, you'd, well, you'd be in big trouble for one thing, but for the other thing, you'd find millions of little fat blobs, a testimony to an unfortunate weakness for all things cheesy. Nachos? Oh yes, please. Triple cheddar burger? I'm swooning here.

But Caesar—and I'm speaking very slowly here on account of you being a moron and all—I know it's bad for me, so I try to remember moderation; hey, it's more than just a river in Egypt. Sorry, wrong aphorism, but you know what I'm trying to say.

Caesar, a boy named Sue who apparently has the brainpower of plankton, claimed that he only recently learned that fast food contains "fat, fat, and more fat" and that since nobody else in his family ever had heart and blood pressure problems it must have been the fast food that did him in.

No, my fat friend, it was *you* who did yourself in, and you alone. Trust me, next time you go into court to pursue this idiotic lawsuit, promise me you won't show up with special sauce on your chin and a taco wrapper stuck to your flip-flop. Could damage your credibility.

To discourage silly lawsuits like the one filed by our fat friend, the National Highway Traffic Safety Administration (youthful new motto: "Safety When*ever*") recently came up with a list of Dangerous Foods You Shouldn't Eat While Driving.

The study came about after an insurance company ordered one of its clients to keep anything edible out of reach while driving because of a history of food-related wrecks. And who said Delta Burke had dropped out of the public eye?

The list was topped by coffee, which not only spills a lot but also can cause serious burns and "therefore, distract drivers who are trying to drive while in pain."

Wouldn't you just pull off the road? What's up with this scenario—drive, sip, spill, oweeeeiiiieee! Drive, sip, spill, whoa! I'm gonna need a graft on that left thigh. Drive, sip, spill . . .

Second on the list was hot soup. Who eats soup while driving? I can barely eat it without spilling while seated in a restaurant armed with the latest ergonomically designed spoon ("Do not use spoon to zing food into another's face, no matter how funny this strikes you"). Just last week, the steroidal crouton in my French onion soup landed in my lap. At least in the car, no one else would've seen it.

Third on the list was tacos. Sure, you're thinking harmless deep-fried tortilla shell stuffed with zesty meat, cheese, and lettuce, but that's just because you don't work in traffic safety. That little half-moon of heaven, when eaten at the wheel, is as deadly as an extended version of the World Music Awards.

Hamburgers made the list because the grease and condiments (I thought grease *was* a condiment) can muck up your hands and the steering wheel. Ditto for fried chicken, jelly doughnuts, and chocolate, which sounded like a mighty satisfying lunch to me.

While I may never injure myself in a doughnut-related traffic mishap, I must tell you that some of those product warnings are a good idea.

How many times I've snickered at those circle-slash pictures of fat babies crawling into containers of joint compound. I mean, who expects the baby to be patching the wallboard anyway? You can't hardly get a baby to do any damn thing around the house.

But, to tell y'all the truth, now I think maybe the fat-baby warning isn't so dumb after all.

How do I know? Well, it happened to me. Sort of. Suffice to say, hons, your garbage can is out to get you and there's no slash-circle to warn you. I'm talking about the big rolling garbage cart, the mean green one. "Green Boy" has always understood my needs; it always gets filled up, but is never too full. It's practically a Zen thing. Up until recently, we had the perfect relationship.

The trouble started when I decided to clean Green Boy, who had developed an unsatisfactory funk following a backyard shrimp-a-roo. I rolled him into the driveway, hooked up the hose, and fetched a bottle of Lysol and scrub mop. Minutes later, the cart, which is chest high to me, was brimming with gallons of soapy water. I scrubbed the sides and top for several satisfying minutes. Still, I wasn't quite sure the bottom was squeaky clean.

I leaned over to scrub the bottom right corner just a . . . little . . . harder.

And that's when my friend turned on me. Literally. Apparently having some sort of acid flashback to being lifted and dumped that morning, the cart snatched me up. My whole body flew into the can with only my feet sticking up. My legs pumped wildly in the air. I couldn't breathe underwater, of course, so I had to rock the can back and forth until GB released me, Jonah-and-the-whale style, spewing my bruised and cut self into the rocks of the alley.

I had bruises, several goose eggs, and a deep gash on my knee, plus I smelled just like a nursing home. Meanwhile, Green Boy just lay on his side, his lid slightly open in what appeared to be a smirk.

So, yes, sometimes you should scare consumers to get their attention. What I would've given for a circle-slash depicting a fat-assed, middle-aged mom upside down in a garbage can.

Sometimes, the dangers are far less obvious than shampooing and drying your hair at the same time. Thank heavens for warnings like I saw in the form of a quarter-page newspaper ad I read the other day: *"Warning!!!* Due to the toilet laws, there are tremendous flushing problems in the United States."

Hons, I haven't been this frightened since I saw myself in Pleather pants. Toilet laws? What toilet laws? Who came up with that and how many of them have I personally violated? (I'm guessing at least six; many more for Caesar.) Anyway, the ad invited the public to a two-hour seminar in which they would have the chance to "witness firsthand the world-famous flushing performance of Toto brand toilets."

(Like you, I'm wondering how they demonstrated that exactly. Did a slick salesman invite the fattest fellow around to chow down on a few Taco Bell gorditas ["remove paper wrapper before eating"] and say, "Heh-heh, let's just see what develops.")

When I calmed myself down, I realized I don't have to worry about this because I live in an eighty-year-old house with original plumbing, therefore my toilets use hundreds, perhaps thousands, of gallons of water with each flush.

Though personally unaffected by the "tremendous flushing problems" threatening our nation's BM security, I'm in no need of a toilet named after a small irksome arm dog. Still, I worry about the rest of y'all. So sue me.

Epilogue

*W*hen *I* started writing the essays in this book, my daughter was two years old and I still had my right mind. Okay, that's an exaggeration; she was probably closer to three.

Anywho, as they say in the South (like saying "buddy-ro!" at the end of a sentence for emphasis, we don't know why we say it, we just do), that's only been two years ago but finding the time to write has been tougher than woodpecker lips. I once read that Maya Angelou rents a motel room to write her poetry so she won't have any distractions, a secret room that only she knows about. What a wuss, I thought. It doesn't really count unless you're writing with a kid on your lap, two cats clawing at the hem of your robe every time you cross your legs, and constant calls from telemarketers who want to sell you everything short of a new pair of lungs.

As I kept writing, however, I started seeing Maya's point. (Although—and this is just a personal opinion—I don't care where she writes but I sure do wish she'd make her poems *rhyme* like God intended.)

Unlike my twenty years working in newsrooms, working from home has had its own set of distractions and, well, loneliness. In the newsroom, you could always walk away and find a real live grown-up (excluding the sports guys) to talk to, and don't forget the lure of the office vending machines, all lined up and waiting to serve. No "hairy raspberry Twinkies" beckon me at home like they did at the office.

For the most part, writing this book has been exhilarating, exhausting, and everything in between. I wouldn't be the first to compare writing a book to the birth process but I swear it's the truth. The only difference is that there's not some nice starched lady patting your hand and feeding you little feel-great pills at the end of the process.

I think I've learned a lot while working from home and making the switch from full-time newsie to stay-at-home mom/newspaper columnist. Most importantly, I learned that you can actually buy those fabulous hairy raspberry things at the grocery store. Who knew?

But as much as I've learned about working from home, I confess the whole mommy thing continues to mystify

me. I see others handle it with such grace and skill. Me?
I still freak out when the little girl in my daughter's class
picks her nose and rubs snot on my sweater before running away squealing. (Okay, actually it's *me* running way
squealing.) My PTA legacy may be that I'm the only
mommy who ever tried to cut corners and make the cor-
nucopia for the class Thanksgiving party using canned
vegetables.

That's why I'm so grateful to know so many competent
mommies. They're the ones who handle booger attacks
with calm acceptance, smiling kindly while simultane-
ously reaching for the wipes that magically appear from
somewhere, perhaps their Superior Mommy gills.

Truthfully, I'm proud to know these women, great
strong Southerner women who can hoe a garden in the
morning and teach cotillion classes in the afternoon. And
I adore our Southern men, too. Contrary to popular opinion, they're not just NASCAR-obsessed mullet-heads.
Not that there's anything wrong with that.

With men and women like that, there's no shortage
of material. As a newspaper columnist, I used to point
my old Dodge down a different highway four days a week
trying to find someone to write about. It was cake, hons.
One day a pair of elderly nightgown-wearing sisters who
made clothes out of Budweiser cans; the next I'd meet
a woman who spoke in pure poetry (listen up, Maya)

when she discussed why she loved hanging her "warsh" out to dry on the clothesline.

That's the thing about Southerners. It may seem silly to some, but we can actually get misty-eyed about sun-scented sheets and towels.

When I recently closed up the small country house I grew up in, I was honestly touched that everybody I called—the gas company, the water department, and so on—all said, "Oh, we're gonna miss y'all. Stay in touch, you hear?"

Can you imagine having that kind of conversation anywhere but a tiny Southern town where—I swear—the town's one limousine service also collects the garbage every week after they fold down the seats and vacuum out the rice and rose petals?

I actually grew up in a town where it was possible that you might get your trash picked up, go to the prom, and get married all using the same vehicle.

And, in the words of that great mentally challenged Southern man, Forrest Gump, that's all I got to say about that.

Acknowledgments

I can't imagine having a more dedicated literary agent than Jenny Bent, whose tenacity, sincerity, and humor made this book possible. I am grateful as all get out to her, and to sure-handed editor Jennifer Enderlin of St. Martin's Press, whose skill and wisdom have made this book the best it could be.

I'm also indebted to the (Myrtle Beach, SC) *Sun News*, and editors Gwen Fowler and Carolyn Murray, who always make me feel like I'm part of the team, even though I'm writing from home, ninety miles away.

In equal amounts, I am indebted to funny friends who continue to inspire and rejuvenate me. Making me laugh on a regular basis are the incomparable Lisa Noecker, Esq. and David Willard, the two funniest Southerners I know.

ACKNOWLEDGMENTS

I'm grateful to longtime friends Gray Wells and Pam Sander who have always, always been there for me; to Nan Graham and Betsy Pollard, my go-to belles for knowledge of all things Southern; to Clifton Truman Daniel, my very favorite Yankee; and to Joy Allen, publisher of *Greater Wilmington Business* magazine.

Praise be to the wonderful, insightful, supportive "mommies," who have kept me sane (sort of) and centered for years: Angela Stilley, Page Rutledge, Dana Sachs, Jana Moore, Tish Baker, Amy MacKay, Michelle Powell, and Susan Pleasants.

Finally, for unabashed encouragement and a steady flow of story ideas, I give thanks to my family: my parents, Howard and Caroline Rivenbark; my sister, Stephanie Rivenbark; my sisters-in-law, Linda and Judy Whisnant; my mother-in-law, Nancy Whisnant; "Uncle" John Bell; Aunt Rachel; and my niece and nephew, Lucy and Nathan Bell.

Most especially, I am grateful for the love and support of my adorable husband, Scott Whisnant, a gifted writer and editor his own self, and of our beloved daughter, Sophie, who will surely despise me when I start writing about her teenage years, but, for now, thinks I hung the moon that we say good night to. I love you all.

READING GROUP GUIDE

1. Although written from a Southern woman's perspective, do you believe that most of the book's comic themes translate easily to non-Southerners? In other words, do Minnesota dads also have difficulty dressing their children properly?

2. The author admits that she adores Southern men, even the mullet headed ones. What characteristics do they possess that you find charming and endearing? Which traits do you find dated and exasperating?

3. The author paints a portrait of the Southern woman as a highly competitive creature. What cultural or historical influences may have led to this trait? Why do you think so many Southern women compete in beauty pageants, talent contests, and even recipe contests?

4. Do you find the slow and soft speech pattern of Southerners irritating or charming? Do you think that a slow drawl indicates that the speaker is a bit dim? Do you believe that a woman's Southern drawl can be used effectively to manipulate others, particularly men?

5. There are many references to being "raised right." Do you believe that Southerners are more apt to punish their children than non-Southern parents? Why or why not?

6. So many non-Southerners derive their knowledge of what Southern folk are like by the images on TV and in films. What are the most memorable Southern characters you recall? Do you think that Hollywood perpetuates a stereotype that Southerners are lazy and slow? Can you remember any major movies in which the brainy heroine is a Southern woman?

7. This book is called "laugh-out-loud funny." Which part made you laugh out loud and why? Does the author's humor remind you of anyone else? How so?

8. Although this book resonates with women readers more than men, many women have read aloud portions to their husbands and boyfriends. Are there specific parts of the book that you think appeal to men?

For more reading group suggestions visit
www.stmartins.com/smp/rgg.html

 St. Martin's Griffin